The
TEACHER'S CALLING

The Teacher's Calling:

A Spirituality for Those Who Teach

Gloria Durka

PAULIST PRESS
New York/Mahwah, N.J.

Cover design by Ray Lundgren

Book design by Joseph E. Petta

Library of Congress Cataloging-in-Publication Data

Durka, Gloria.
    The teacher's calling : a spirituality for those who teach / by Gloria Durka.
        p.   cm.
    Includes bibliographical references (p.   ).
    ISBN 0-8091-4062-4 (alk. paper).
        1. Teaching—Religious aspects—Christianity. 2. Teachers—Religious life. 3. Education—Aims and objectives. 4. Spiritual life. I. Title.
LB1027.2 .D87 2002
371.102—dc21

                                                                                    2001055425

Published by Paulist Press
997 Macarthur Boulevard
Mahwah, New Jersey 07430

www.paulistpress.com

Printed and bound in the
United States of America

CONTENTS

For Jack
(John R. McCall, Ph.D.)

TEACHER

"...what we have loved, others will love, and we will teach them how...."
—William Wordsworth

Introduction

There is something mysterious and fascinating about teaching. The longer we do it, the more we become aware that we can never fully know our students or the subjects we teach. The more we think about them, the more clearly we see the limits of our understanding. This insight has been called the "learned uncertainty of teachers." And yet, there is at the same time a deepening awareness that there is much that we do know about this mysterious activity. For example, we become more convinced that texts and common human experience have something to teach us and that even though their meanings appear to be inexhaustible, we can discern their interpretations. Through our commitment to inquiry, we can discern which interpretations really are better than others and which can help our students and us to become more fully human. Teachers who are aware of their call to preserve and transmit our traditions as sources of beauty, truth and freedom are less likely to be bored, dull or tired. It is my hope that this modest book can affirm in some measure the role of teachers as ministers of personal and social transformation, and that it might help readers to celebrate the mystery and wonders of a teacher's calling.

CHAPTER 1

Teaching from the Heart:
The Soul of the Teacher

When did you first know that you wanted to be a teacher? Was it a decision you came to quickly, or did it emerge gradually over time? Perhaps you still wonder why you are teaching or why you are still teaching. Such questions are not easily answered, and they usually are pondered for years. They are not simply questions about our job, although they include job-related issues: They are questions about our soul's life and work. For this reason, teaching cannot merely be treated as a routine job—it flows from an inner incentive. Teaching is more a vocation than a job, and it is much easier to change jobs than it is to switch vocations. Perhaps that is why many of us have taught several different grade levels, subjects and students in a variety of settings. Through the diversity of our teaching experience, we have probably realized that our vocation is expressed over time. In fact, we may teach for years before we genuinely begin to feel it as a vocation and treat it as such. It takes a while for us to realize just how much our work embodies our vision of teaching and our beliefs about students. We grow to understand that teaching is a calling that makes claims on our souls.

There has been a great deal of research showing that many people enter teaching for idealistic reasons. They want to work with youth, to have a positive influence on others and to pass on what they know and care about. Research also shows that successful teachers conceive their work in broader terms than in the simple accomplishment of a function. Otherwise, it would be easy to give into the temptation just to "cover" the material mechanically, to accept low expectations of one's students or to abandon society's expectations and just do what one pleases.

Teaching is not simply a profession. As most teachers soon discover, there has been a long struggle in the professional world to gain respect for teaching. Professions are recognized by outside criteria. Standards of qualification, performance and evaluation are established by professional organizations and institutions to assist in the selection of appropriate candidates for teaching positions. But there is an important difference between *profession* and *vocation*. People can conduct themselves professionally but may not consider their work a calling. Those who regard teaching as a vocation derive their identity from an inner motivation that allows them to shape their roles rather than merely occupy them. Also, the idea of *profession* stresses public recognition, greater autonomy and larger rewards, whereas *vocation* focuses inward to the core of the practice itself. The sense of vocation, then, finds expression at the crossroad of public obligation and personal fulfillment. But vocation cannot exist as a state of mind alone.

Vocation presumes a sense of adventure to engage the world. Teaching as a vocation presumes a hopeful, outward-looking attitude of devoting oneself to the activities of teaching that stem from the inner urge to venture out and devote oneself to working firsthand. In other words, a sense of adventure with all of its unpredictability and uncertainty is inherent in the notion of teaching as a vocation. Somehow, to teach requires that we jump in with gusto, eager to begin again—even with some measure of panic! To *devote* oneself to teaching is to be true to one of the original meanings of the word *vocation,* which is, "to commit *oneself in an enduring way to a particular practice*" [italics added].[1]

Teaching is more than selfless devotion. To say that teaching is a vocation might conjure up notions of asceticism or other associations with Christian belief and practice. Some of the ideas are from early Christianity, but they were modified during the Reformation that began in the sixteenth century. Vocation came to express a secular calling, one into which one was born and which was to be carried out in a spirit of service to Christian and ethical aims. Puritans, for example, distinguished between a "general" and a "particular" calling. A "general" calling meant being called to a Christian way of life regardless of one's secular occupation. The "particular" vocation was the specific activity in which one worked.

Today, some teachers also distinguish between a general and particular call. For example, one can separate the feeling of being called to teach from a desire to teach a particular subject or age level of students. That is, one can separate the desire, "I want to be a teacher," from "I want to teach primary school reading" or "I want to teach high school religion." Some of us soon discover that strictly occupational language is inadequate for describing why we teach, and we may find ourselves using language with spiritual overtones so that we feel compelled to speak of our hopes for our students and our faith in their future. We tend to self-describe what we do, not so much in language of self-denial, but in the language of creativity, engagement, imagination and transformation.

Teaching is always more than a personal matter. Our inner motivations are important, but they are only a part of the story of teaching. One cannot simply "have a vocation" in the abstract. Rather, it is a set of impulses that are outward looking and outward moving, focused on what calls one to act. The idea of teaching as a vocation presumes a social reality in which to work out the inner desire to contribute to the transformation of the world. The practice "calls" the teacher. We teach for the good of the community.

A teacher's calling is active and compelling. The practice of teaching is a social event. If a person feels called to teach but has no place or means to teach, the call remains fruitless. We can respond to the call to teach because there is a practice of teaching with requirements and responsibilities. The response to the call is not simply a passive event. Something about teaching is larger than the person, something that whets the appetite, captures the imagination, makes one desire to do something. The source of that call is not just *within* the person, but one's own teachers, experiences of working with youngsters in an educational capacity or the example of acquaintances who are teachers usually spark it. The response to the call is sparked from without. Person and practice are interdependent, much like public service and personal fulfillment.

Each teacher's vocation is unique. Even though there are common threads in the calling of each teacher, each teacher dwells in the role in a unique way. We each give our vocation a distinctive personal stamp. The individual who occupies the role of teacher makes all the difference. If we can see ourselves as noninterchangeable with others, we can enrich what we do with more significance. We are more like architects than laborers, more like artists than mechanics. We not only strive to gain the skills necessary to do our work but we strive to know better those for whom we do our work. Our work is a common work that we do in a unique way.

Teaching has an old English root, *taecan*, which means "to share, to instruct," or more literally, to provide signs or outward expressions of something one knows. Such teaching is a form of public service to others, and at the same time it provides a person with a sense of identity and personal fulfillment. Such teaching is a vocation.

Living and Working in Ordinariness

To regard our teaching as a vocation does not mean that we at last can fully appreciate what our commitment means. Our commitment to teaching can (and probably does!) coexist with lifelong questions and doubts. Even after years of teaching we can still wonder about how teaching really "happens" or about whether we are truly fit for the work. We all know that the work is full of surprises. There are lessons that lead to unexpected insights and questions. There are students who learn and grow. And there are lessons that seem to fail even though we have planned them ever so carefully and with great thoroughness. There are the students who seem bored or "stuck." What is amazing is how any person could willingly embrace such a flood of joy, disappointment, surprise, sadness and delight. These emotions are part of the routine rhythm of teaching.

The sense of teaching as a vocation involves a measure of determination, courage and flexibility rather than a sense of heroism. The teacher's calling is sustained by a sense that the work of teaching is an activity whose meaning is larger than the sum of its parts. It is larger than carrying out numerous duties, responsibilities and mundane or routine tasks. We do these things because they are somehow necessary and, although they are not especially rewarding, we are able to press on...and on. We have to tidy up our classrooms, prepare our lessons, keep our materials in order, read and evaluate student papers, attend to many students' questions, file reports and much more.

While these activities, taken together over time, can be blamed for draining our energy and undermining our enthusiasm for teaching, it is possible to take a different view. Just as the ordinary tasks of living (cooking, eating, housekeeping, etc.) can be a burden sometimes, they are at the same time the tasks that give us a sense of rhythm, balance, direction and engagement in life. As long as it is possible for us to delight in baking a loaf of bread, preparing a meal for friends or family, or resting in a freshly cleaned room, we will not be overwhelmed by the physical energy such tasks require. While we may tire, the realization that we will be refreshed by rest can sustain us. The cycle of living promises us peace and contentment. So the routine obligations of teaching need not distract us from our sense of vocation; they can be regarded as very necessary parts of it. We don't have to enjoy every minute of drudgery, but we can regard them as part of the larger work we do. Indeed, for most of us, it is through the everyday aspects of teaching that we mold connections with our students, and this in turn can bring to life our sense of vocation.

Believing in the Ordinary

Sometimes the conditions in which we teach are less than ideal—even bleak. The physical environment may be poor— we may not have all that we need to teach certain lessons effectively; the socioeconomic environment may be charged with loss and diminishment—high levels of poverty, low employment, dangerous neighborhoods, stressful family situations. Research has shown that many beginning teachers leave the classroom after a few years. Many leave for understandable reasons. A frequently cited reason is the difficulty teachers have of adjusting their hopes and dreams with the reality of working with large numbers of students who bring varying degrees of interest and readiness to learn. Some leave teaching because they are overwhelmed by the lack of institutional support for their efforts.

A sense of our calling can keep us on course. If we believe, in the depths of our souls, that what we do in the classroom makes a difference in the lives of those we teach, we can live and work in a different world from that which meets the eye. We can inhabit a world in which we see youngsters with many strikes against them who have a great deal to learn about life and about getting along with others. This is the world in which we must believe and act as if our efforts as teachers are significant and worthwhile. This conviction can enable us to work patiently and persistently with youngsters whom many other teachers find unbearable. Our way of life embodies the belief that the improvement of self and of human life are always worth whatever it takes to create a better world for all. Of those who see this as folly, we dare to ask, "What would it be like to teach without such conviction?" We do what we do because we believe that doing it, even in the most trying of conditions, is better than *not* doing it. This belief and these efforts lie at the heart of what being a teacher is all about.

Of course, teachers can let their perceptions be influenced, even determined, by others. But they can also influence their perceptions through reflection and through their own actions. As tomes of research on teaching demonstrate, the personal fulfillment one can derive from taking risks is great, but so are the unanticipated frustrations and difficulties. Even so, most teachers describe an increased sense of commitment to teaching, not a diminished sense. Perhaps you have had that experience as well. Perhaps as you recognized what teaching could mean, you saw larger possibilities in it for being a force for good, and you became much more engaged with teaching. Perhaps as your own understanding of your calling as a teacher took shape, so too did your awareness that you could push yourself further, that you had neither exhausted nor even fully discovered your own capacity to teach. It is this *sense that one has something to contribute, that one can make a difference, and that one can shape the world and not just be shaped by it* that shows the power of a sense of vocation. Finding success with some of our students attests to the practical value of our desire to serve. We would do well to find ways to celebrate these moments with one another.

Such a sense of vocation is not a set of glasses or lenses that we can take off and put on at will. It is not an arbitrary way of looking at life. Such a way of looking at life is a result of our character that has been formed over time. It flows from our soul.

Reflection: Teaching from Your Heart

Some things to think about from EXPERIENCE:

In his book, *The Courage to Teach*, Parker Palmer writes:

> Teaching, like any truly human activity, emerges from one's inwardness, for better or worse. As I teach, I project the condition of my soul onto my students, my subject and our way of being together. The entanglements I experience in the classroom are no more or less than the convolutions of my inner life. Viewed from this angle, teaching holds a mirror to my soul. If I am willing to look in that mirror, and not run from what I see, I have a chance to gain self-knowledge—and knowing myself is as crucial to good teaching as knowing my students and my subject.[2]

- Does this ring true for you? In what ways?
- Can you recall any times when things didn't go well in class because you were upset or distracted before you began teaching?

- Have you noticed any connection between feeling good yourself with what happens in the classroom?
- Do you think anyone can separate the teaching from the teacher? Consider the following to help your reflection:

> O chestnut-tree, great-rooted blossomer,
> Are you the leaf, the blossom or the bole?
> O body swayed to music, O brightening glance,
> How can we know the dancer from the dance?[3]
> —W. B. Yeats

- Does this poem speak to you in any way about yourself and your teaching?
- Do any specific incidents come to mind that give you clues about teaching from your heart?
- It has been written that

> Knowing others is intelligence,
> knowing yourself is true wisdom.
> Mastering others is strength;
> mastering yourself is true power.[4]
> —Lao-Tzu

Do you agree?

Some things to think about from the SCRIPTURES:

Earlier in this chapter, the claim was made that "We are more like architects than laborers, more like artists than mechanics." Think about this claim as you ponder the following:

> We are fellow workers with God; you are God's farm, God's building....By the grace God gave me, I succeeded as an architect and laid the foundations, on which someone else is doing the building. Everyone doing the building must work carefully. For the foundation, nobody can

lay any other than the one which has already been laid, that is Jesus Christ. On this foundation you can build in gold, silver and jewels, or in wood, grass and straw, but whatever the material, the work of each builder is going to be clearly revealed when the day comes.

(1 Cor 3:9–13 NJB)

Can you make any connections with this text and the work of teaching? Spend a few moments rereading each phrase and thinking about your own passion for teaching.

Or, you might repeat this phrase at the beginning and end of the passage:

"You study my heart...." "Teach me your way, Yahweh, and I will obey you faithfully; give me an undivided heart...."

(Ps 17:3; Ps 86:11)

Praying about Teaching:

I thank you, Yahweh, with all my heart;
I sing praise to you before the angels.
I worship at your holy temple and praise your name
because of your constant
love and faithfulness
Because you have shown that you and your words are
   exalted
You answered me when I called to you;
you built up strength within me.
All the rulers of the earth will praise you, Yahweh,
because they have heard your promises.
They will sing about your ways
and about your great glory.
Even though you are exalted,
You care for the lowly.
The proud cannot hide from you.
Even when I am surrounded by troubles,
you keep me safe;

you oppose my angry enemies
and save me by your power.
You will do everything you have promised me;
Yahweh, your faithful love endures forever.
Complete the work that you have begun.

(Ps 138)

CHAPTER 2

Teaching Courageously: Showing How

Facing each new class at the beginning of the school year or semester is an act of courage. But after years of teaching, the kind of courage it requires changes. Early on, we need courage simply to show up and face our students, and then to discipline them, to motivate them to work and to dare them to do better. The longer we teach, the deeper the courage we need. As we grow in understanding of our calling, we look at each new class and know that we must let each of these young people into our life in some significant way. The issue is one of heart. Can we open our hearts to thirty more third graders, two hundred more adolescents or fifty more graduate students? Put bluntly, can we love enough to open ourselves up to another batch of strangers?

It doesn't get easier with time because each new encounter makes unique demands on us. Each situation is new. It is not as though we have been teaching for fifteen years and keep repeating the activities of teaching fifteen times. Rather, we have had fifteen different experiences.

When I was preparing to be a teacher, a wise professor told us to throw out our plan books at the end of each year.

She told us not to be tempted to save them under the pretense that they would be helpful to us the following year. She stressed that each new group of students was unique, and all of our fashioning of curriculum and activities should be done to meet *their* needs. To this day, I heed her words. I am convinced that doing so helps to keep my teaching fresh.

We can learn a lot about courage from other teachers: for example, seeing how another teacher welcomes a refugee child; noticing a teacher's gentle tone with an unruly student; observing a colleague staying after school to tutor a teenager who "just can't seem to get it"; watching a colleague patiently explaining a point of instruction; admiring the even temper of one who tries to resolve student conflict; and admiring the fidelity of those who come to class in spite of a bad headache or having to leave a sick child at home in someone else's care. Where does such courage come from? It comes from generosity of heart.

Generosity of heart allows teachers to watch their students move beyond them, thinking and writing better than they themselves have ever done. We can admire those teachers who send their students to colleges they themselves could never afford and are happy for them, not jealous of them. Such teachers have learned generosity of heart; we can learn it, too.

Knowing How

Can a person be taught how to teach? Are good teachers "born," not made? Studies of model teachers have shown that sound instructional methods are necessary in teaching. Teaching without good methodology, without an understanding of what you are and what you can do, is like "trying to paint without a brush and colors." You need more than technique to be an artist; you need vision. *Technique* or *method* can be described as a way of "doing" reality. This "doing" flows from a way of "seeing" reality. The teacher is one who brings a particular vision of the world to share with the students.

There are various perspectives to education. It can be regarded as a process of initiating young people into the ways of thinking and behaving characteristic of the culture into which they were born. In another perspective, it is the development of a person from innocence to experience, from the limitations of childish immediacies to the open possibilities of conceptual thought. In yet another, it is the effort of a community to recreate itself with the rise of each new generation and to perpetuate itself in historic time.[1]

No matter how a teacher regards education, the primary task is to teach the young how to know. Schools have traditionally been understood as places where knowledge is transmitted, where children are exposed to views of the world accepted by their culture and where beliefs and truths are taught. Students are more than "human resources" for greater productivity and economic gain. They come to us with questions and frustrations, dreams and anxieties, hopes and fears. Some are restless; others appear blank. We find ourselves daring them to break with their given views, that which is taken for granted—to move toward what might be, what is not yet, what is possible. How can our methods serve such a purpose? One thing is clear: No matter how polished a method is, it will accomplish nothing without someone to use it—one who is just as active, interested, engaged and curious about the reasoning behind a method as about the steps it contains.

Our sense of vocation brings methods of teaching to life and renders them in the service of life. Methodology is not just a way to socialize students into a way of life, keep them under control or pass along information. Knowing the subject matter well is also not enough to guarantee effective teaching. A teacher's sense of vocation is related to his or her commitment to intellectual self-improvement and subsequently to that of their students. Vocation without skill is ineffective, but skills without a sense of service can be superficial.

Passion for the Possible

How are we to serve our students in their quest for a meaningful life? How can we provide the means for them to live in peace amidst diversity? The world is broken in so many places with shattered communities and lives. For starters, we can believe that it is possible to move the young from *what is* to *what is not yet*. Such belief requires a good measure of passion. Passion has been called the *power* of possibility. This is so because it is the source of our interests and our purposes that signifies mood, emotion, desire— modes of grasping the appearance of things. It is a way of recognizing possibility, "the presence of the future as that which is lacking and that which, by its very absence, reveals reality."[2] We need to nourish our own sense of the possible. A good place to begin is to reflect on our own attitude toward taking risks.

Are we willing to try something new, to experiment, to try out a new idea? Or are we more prone to choose what has worked for us before or something that others have already done? Do we need to have control more than adventure? Some writers on education contrast *objective knowledge* with *primitive knowledge*. With objective knowledge we try to own and control reality, and by so doing we turn everything, including nature and human beings, into objective things.

Primitive knowledge is based on feeling, intuition and faith. Formal education in our culture largely portrays the self as *knower* and the world as *known*. Knowledge is derived from "facts" and the process of education consists in "finding the facts." Such a separation of knower and known, learner and the material to be learned, is now seriously questioned. Philosophers of science, for example, suggest that every scientific finding is a mixture of the objective and subjective. In other words, the very notion of *truth* is being refined. Parker Palmer points out that the word *truth* is derived from a Germanic root that gives rise to our word *troth,* as in the ancient vow "I pledge my troth." He says, "With this word one person enters a covenant with another, a pledge to engage in a mutually accountable and transforming relationship, a relationship forged of trust and faith in the face of unknowable risks."[3] If we shape our classrooms by this understanding of truth, we can gather facts, share knowledge and test different interpretations against one another. The conflicts that result will allow fuller knowledge to come out. The classroom is formed by the truth that emerges from the interdependence of the knowers and the subject matter.

When we regard teaching as a "dance" between the knowers and the material, it is easier to rethink our own roles. First, it becomes clearer that we are to create a space in which truth is neither suppressed nor merely accepted. The focus is not on instant answers but rather on adventure, wrestling with untruth, silence and listening. Palmer calls this atmosphere *hospitality,* "where everyone is accepted, when one can expose ignorance, express feelings, try out new hypotheses, challenge other ideas and engage in mutual criticism."[4]

Second, we are responsible for maintaining contact with the transcendent center that calls into being and shapes a community of diverse individuals into an organic, interrelated and mutually responsive body. In other words, by focusing on the subject matter (letting the subjects speak for themselves) in the spirit and practice of prayer and *meditation* and by being mindful of the gathered students and of the teacher, deep learning occurs. Of course, the developmental level of the group will influence this learning. But the goal is shared by children, youth and adults: openness to and empathy with *others* who are different; interdependence; respect for one another's rights; *internalization* of authority; shared wisdom in the ongoing search for truth.

Certainly, in the classroom the teacher is the primary academic resource that is required to evaluate and document the performance of students. The teacher (who is also a learner) is not the same as the student. While there can be genuine dialogue in a classroom, it does not mean that there is equal power in it. The teacher has the responsibility for designing the environment and for guiding the process of education.

Teaching by Design

What we do as we strive to teach with a *passion for the possible* is more than just shaping. As Gabriel Moran puts it, "all attempts to shape human life are reshapings of past achievements."[5] He goes on to say that for a human learner, "shaping is of the human organism in relation to its environment. This relation already has a shape so that a teacher can only help to reshape what is given." Moran suggests the term *design* because it attempts to capture both the expressed intent of the human teacher and the material limits of what can be taught. For him, design is a more precise image than shape. I agree.

Shaping is a term that implies a preexisting thing to be worked upon. The emphasis is on the thing or object. *Design,* on the other hand, has to do with an activity. As Moran points out, "the potential learner is doing something; to teach is to change what is being done."[6] All teaching-learning is by doing. Aristotle highlighted this insight when he observed that there is only one activity in teaching, and it is in the learner. Across the whole range of human learning, Aristotle sees an underlying principle: "Men become builders by building and lyre players by playing the lyre, so too we become just by doing just acts, and brave by doing brave acts."[7] So as long as we teach, we are students of teaching. We become better teachers by teaching—or at least we should!

Teaching by design includes *instruction*. Indeed, instruction has a central place in teaching. It does not impede human freedom. Anyone who wishes to learn needs instruction. Good instruction is precisely directed at the elements of the skill involved. As a student masters the skill, he or she will find ways to go beyond the instruction or to work variations within the instruction. But here is a key point: Instruction is a highly directive act. It is intentional and specific. So, as Moran concludes, a good teacher is one who "shows how."

We simply cannot escape that responsibility—we are obliged to instruct. This aspect of teaching will be explored further in chapter 5. For now I wish to stress that a passionate commitment for the possible does not mean "anything goes." Rather, it means that we intentionally strive to use every measure of creativity that we can muster to inspire and lure our students to awaken their own spirits. Consequently, modeling is central to teaching.

Designing a Holy Work

In his poem, "Leaves of Grass," Walt Whitman writes:

I am the poet of the Body and I am the poet of the Soul....[8]

There is much to drink from the fountain of his work. His words in this line remind us of absence, ambiguity and embodiments of existential possibility. They call us to reflect on our work as companion-tutors, an ancient notion of how teachers do their work. The tutor, or *paedagogus*, was a slave who accompanied the student to school, sat through the lessons and drilled the student on the lessons when he returned home. Being a tutor meant sharing the schooling with the student and leading the student to the full meaning of the lessons learned.

Being a *companion* is being someone who nourishes the heart, mind, soul and body of those with whom we walk. The word *companion* comes from two Latin words: *com,* meaning "with," and *panis,* meaning "bread." Companions are, therefore, people who share bread with others. The bread we share is the bread of becoming more fully human and thus more fully holy.

Clement of Alexandria, toward the end of the second century, described the work of Jesus Christ as that of a *paedagogus.* Those working in the Christian tradition uniquely participate in the work of accompanying students in the process of education. This education is not one that produces lawyers, engineers, computer programmers or the like. Careers, making a living, job specialization are useful, but they are not enough. This is not an education *for* anything; it is an education *of* someone, of a human person. Such a perspective allows us to realize that whatever furthers humanization furthers the work of the church. "The church is the community in which intimate union with God and the unity of all mankind are demonstrated to be identical, because there the identity of the two is lived."[9]

Whatever furthers humanization is the work of the church. Instruction in literature, science, philosophy and social interaction, as well as instruction in religion, is directly related to the work of the church. Whatever makes us more human makes us more like God, whether we explicitly acknowledge this or not, claims the theologian, Michael Himes.[10] When we grasp this insight, we understand our calling as a holy work, and it gives us courage because we do not do it alone. Jesus is our *paedagogus,* our companion-tutor, during this education.

Reflections: Teaching from Your Heart

Some things to think about from EXPERIENCE:

Here is a true story:

> It was a cold January day and Sister Rosalie was adjusting the window shades in her first-grade classroom. In a few minutes the room would be filled with thirty-five youngsters who had just walked to school from the surrounding neighborhood. No school buses here, and no car pools. The neighborhood was inhabited by poor families who knew the meaning of hard work and struggled daily to make ends meet. Many parents worked in the local meat processing plant, others in the dog-and-cat-food factory. Sister Rosalie appreciated the cold weather because somehow the air seemed cleaner, and with the windows shut the desks and floor were cleaner, too. No film from the smoke of the factories covered them.
>
> It was a new week and another chance to try to reach Howie. She was concerned about this little boy who was quieter then the rest of the kids. While the other six-year-olds were reading their primers with great delight and a little flair, Howie resisted reading aloud. He rarely spoke to the other children, and yet Sister Rosalie could see that he watched them. His writing was very irregular, so she expressed to her principal her concern that perhaps Howie had a vision problem. What could the school do to see that Howie got help? Sister Principal said she would look into it. Later that very day, about an hour after school let out, Howie's brother appeared at the convent door. After hesitating a few moments, he rang the bell and sheepishly waited for someone to answer.

Sister Rosalie opened the door and immediately recognized Howie's big brother, who was in the fifth grade. "What can I do for you, Jim?" she asked. After a few false starts and a fair amount of stuttering, Jim blurted out that his mother had told him to come by to see if there was any way the sisters could help them—just for today—because they were short on food. Sister Rosalie was stunned. "In this day and age with food stamps and a variety of family assistance programs, who would ever think that a family would be reduced to sending a child out to beg for food," she thought. "Come right in for a minute, Jim, while I talk to Sister Janita." Sister Rosalie delivered the message to the superior of the house, who was equally surprised: "Tell him to wait a few minutes while we get some things together." Both sisters went into the pantry and filled four bags with groceries. Since there was no way that Jim could carry them himself, the two sisters decided to walk home with him. They made small talk on their way, trying to distract Jim from his obvious embarrassment.

When they arrived on the front porch of the house, Jim ran in, calling out to his mother. The sisters stood outside until she appeared. It was obvious she did not expect to see two nuns on her porch. "Please come in out of the cold," she said as she nervously stepped aside. "These are for you," said Sister Janita, as she handed one of the bags to the mother. Meanwhile, Sister Rosalie looked around with wide eyes. There was no furniture in the living room except for a large television set. Howie was sitting on the floor in front of it. A blanket was off to the side. The wooden floors looked cold and barren. "What were the other rooms like," she wondered, "Do they have beds?" A half hour later, the two sisters were making their way home. They learned that the family had moved into the neighborhood last August. They had come north from another state because they had heard that it was easier to get good jobs here. However, the factories were not hiring so the father was working as a cab driver, and their money ran out—rent, heat, electricity and the new baby all had drained their savings. So they sold some furniture—they were hoping to replace the old stuff anyway—just to get by until things turned the corner. It was obvious that they were proud people.

"We've got work to do," Sister Janita said as they tromped through the snow-covered sidewalks. She proceeded to talk about a list of things that had to get done to help that family: contact family services, call Catholic Charities to get a social worker to visit, gather information on entitlement programs for medical assistance for the new baby and mother, etcetera. But Sister Rosalie could hardly hear it all. She was still thinking of Howie, and her concern for him felt very different from what she felt earlier that morning. She understood her role as teacher in a deeper way than as an instructor in reading and writing, and she felt sure that this understanding would deepen even further as time went on. From learning more about Howie's family life, her eyes opened wider, and she began to see herself as a teacher who is also called to be a companion...literally. Yes, there was a lot of work to do. How could she have ever had "eyes so wide shut?" Yes, *they* had work to do.

- Can you identify with this story in any way?
- Have you known any "Howies"?
- Did you ever have the realization that your eyes were "wide shut"? If so, how did it affect your teaching?
- Can you think of a time when your eyes opened wide? How did it affect your teaching?

There is a Zen saying that goes as follows:

> When the student is ready, the teacher will appear.

- How might this saying be related to the story of Sister Rosalie and Howie?

Ponder this message from Goethe:

> There is one elementary truth the ignorance of which kills countless ideas and splendid plans: the moment one definitely commits oneself then Providence moves, too. All sorts of things occur to help one that never otherwise would have occurred....Whatever you can do or dream, you can do, begin it. Boldness has genius, power and magic in it. Begin it now.[11]

- What does it say to you about teaching?
- Are you bold enough when you teach?

Some things to think about from the SCRIPTURES:

We began this chapter by exploring the need for courage in teaching. The Psalms can give us a clue on where to find the courage we need:

> ...for this I know—that God is with me.
> In God I trust and shall not be afraid.
> (Ps 56, 10–11)

What do these words mean to you?

Praying about Teaching

> Happy those whose strength is in you;
> They have courage to make the pilgrimage!
> (Ps 84:5)

> Make me know your ways, Yahweh;
> teach me your paths.
> Lead me in your truth and teach me
> for you are the God of my salvation.
> (Ps 25:4–5)

CHAPTER 3

Teaching Creatively: Imagining How

The Possible's slow fuse is lit
By the Imagination.[1]
—Emily Dickinson

We who are teachers know something about limits. In our work, we are called to consciously strive against them. There are the limits of the school environment, including material things such as buildings, furnishings, supplies and so forth. The environment includes the milieu, the expectations of administrators, parents and the learners themselves, as well as the broader environment, such as the parish, neighborhood or section of town. Then there are the limits of vision, dreams, hoped-for ends that are the result of poverty, exclusion, exploitation, oppression. When these circumstances are perceived as natural, as a given, there cannot be freedom because people who accept these situations cannot easily imagine a better state of things. Whether we primarily experience tensions because of the physical limitations of our work or because of the deeper differences of ways of looking at the world, such tensions can either severely hamper our efforts or they can serve as incentives to creatively engage the situation in which we find ourselves.

Limitations affect us personally, and they affect the students with whom we work. Our duty as teachers presses us to engage these circumstances and to constantly relearn how to look at the world. We meet our students with all of their histories, and we bring ourselves with our own experience to each encounter. And "We witness every minute the miracle of related experiences, and yet nobody knows better than we do how this miracle is worked, for we are ourselves this network of relationships."[2] It is through the imagination that people reach beyond their situation to the "as if" or the "not yet." And more than that. Imagination, says Virginia Woolf, "brings the severed parts together."[3] It breaks with the monotonous and the boring.

"But the role of the imagination is not to resolve, not to point the way, nor to improve. It is to awaken, to disclose the ordinarily unseen, unheard, and unexpected"[4] claims the philosopher Maxine Greene. How do we improve imagination? By nurturing it.

One of the best-known teachers of the twentieth century is Sylvia Ashton-Warner. For years she worked with Maori children in New Zealand. They came to her schoolroom undisciplined, hostile and angry. These children were reared in homes where violence was commonplace, and they soon learned violent behaviors as a way of protecting themselves. But Ashton-Warner took the good and the bad elements of the children's experience and developed a method of teaching reading that amazed school administrators across New Zealand and eventually the world. She imaginatively found the words that had intense meaning for each child and used them to impart a love of reading: words like "Mummy," "Daddy," "kiss," "frightened," "ghost." Describing her methodology, she wrote, "I reach a hand into the mind of the child, bring out a handful of the stuff I find there, and use that as our first working material. Whether it is good or bad stuff, violent or placid stuff, coloured or dun...."[5] She wrote each child's word for the day on large, tough cards. These words become the stuff of each child's treasured vocabulary, as she said to a child, "...spell one of your words." Each morning the new words go up on the board. It's exciting because no one knows what's coming up. "Wonderful words appear: helicopter, lady's place, cowboy, sore ear, fish and chips, dirt, Captain Marble, mumps, Superman and King of the Rocket Men." Ashton-Warner said that this way she got a real word and the right spelling. And the children delighted in them. Here's one example she wrote about:

> The word "jalopy" made its fascinating appearance the other day. Brian wrote, "I went to town. I came back on a jalopy bus." This word stirred us. The others cross-questioned him on the character of such a bus. It turned out to mean "rackety" and although the word was picked up at once nevertheless they still ask for it to go up on the spelling list. "We haven't had 'jalopy' for spelling lately," Brian says. He loves spelling it, which is what I mean when I say that the drive is the children's own. It's all so merciful on a teacher.[6]

These children were considered uneducable by some and incapable of meeting grade level standards by others. Yet Ashton-Warner was able to teach them.

How did she do it? The Maori were known to be warlike in their behavior. Yet she was able to transform violent backgrounds and behavior into postures of receptivity and joy. Ashton-Warner believed that there is only one answer to destructiveness—creativity. But she knew it was not easy. Observing a cross section of children from different places in New Zealand, she could observe what she called "progress of the one-patterned mind." She lamented the fact that although she had more than seventy fancy-dress costumes, all of the children wanted the same ones: Superman, Rocket Man or cowboy and cowgirl outfits. The classics—Bo-Peep, Peter Pan, etcetera—gathered dust. And she concludes, "It's this sameness in children that can be so boring."[7]

In reflecting on why this is so, Ashton-Warner observes that children are handed ready-made things from birth, so there is no need for them to conceive anything on their own. She concludes that the capacity quickly dries up. So the vast areas of the mind that could have been alive with creativity have to be filled up with nonstop radio (these were the days before there was a TV in each household) and endless chatter. Here was her dilemma: How could she help children grow up to be interesting, caring and creative people?

A conversation with a friend, a university professor, confirmed her fears. She recorded the conversation as follows. She asks,

> "What kind of children arrive at the University to you?" He said, "They're all exactly the same." "But," I said, "How can it be like that? The whole plan of primary education at least is for diversity." "Well," he answered, "they come to me like samples from a mill. Not one can think for himself. I beg them not to serve back to me exactly what I have given them. I challenge them sometimes with wrong statements to provoke at least some disagreement. But even that won't work." "But," I said, "you must confess to about three percent originality." "One in a thousand," he replied. "One in a thousand." I replied: "In the infant room…we still have identity. It's somewhere between my infant-room level and your university level that the story breaks. But I don't think it is the plan of education itself."[8]

Depending on which grade level you teach, the above conversation can either confirm your suspicions or encourage your efforts. In either case, I am convinced that it is never too late to nurture imagination. How we design our work as teachers influences the inner life of our students. Erich Fromm says that "life has an inner dynamism of its own; it tends to grow, to be expressed, to be lived....The more the drive toward life is thwarted, the stronger is the drive toward destruction; the more life is realized, the less is the strength of destructiveness. *Destructiveness is the outcome of unlived life*" [italics added].[9] Living safely in a peaceful world requires imaginative and creative explorations.

Attending to Creative Teaching

We expect our students to "pay attention." How to get them to do so remains a concern no matter what age they are or how much experience we have. Teachers learn a variety of ways to call a room to attention—a bell, a handclap, a gesture. Most probably use their voices. While there might be great activity in a classroom before a lesson begins, we hope to have our students focus on what we have designed for them to learn. It is more than just getting their attention; it is getting them to be still inside that is important so that they can receive the learning experiences. This stillness is more than silence. It is a posture of receptivity for what is to happen next. Sylvia Ashton-Warner used to play the first eight notes from Beethoven's Fifth Symphony to get her students' attention. It served her well for years. She taught her "little ones" to stop whatever they were doing and look at her when they heard that melody. It never failed. She never spoke until all the children looked at her. How did the children who were busy with all kinds of activities hear those eight notes? If you have taught little ones, you know how. The ones who were near the piano heard the melody, and they would touch others and tell them so that by the time the piano strings had come to rest, so had the children. Remarkable—and possible. What great discipline!

For what do we wish our students to be focused? Is it to make our own job easier? Is it to "cover the material" better? To get good results on standardized or required tests? Why do we do what we do? While all of these might have their place, teachers who understand their calling in religious terms have nourished habits of attention and devotion that have taught them to accept, to receive and to understand the world as well as to seek occasionally to transform and improve it. Being more thoughtful fills us with insight about important matters of human concern and the notion of being considerate of others. One of the characters in Toni Morrison's novel *Beloved* describes what such teaching can mean for our students when he describes his relationship with a particular woman: "She is a friend of my mind. She gather me, man. The pieces I am, she gather them and give them back to me all in the right order. It's good, you know, when you got a woman who is a friend of your mind."[10]

This is another way to think about nurturing our students' minds. It is becoming a friend of someone else's mind, with the wonderful power to return a sense of wholeness to that person. Often, imagination can bring severed parts together and create wholes. The Maori children came to recognize the rhythm of the classroom, and it gave them the opportunities to break with hard realities of the given and stretch toward new possibilities. They recognized various moments of the process of learning. They trusted the teacher and the process to release their imagination, to open new perspectives, to see connections, to see through new lenses.

Discipline invites us to adopt high expectations of our students, regardless of what others might be doing. Such teaching depends far more on what we bring to it than on the kind of resources available to us. Some of us face strenuous burdens and constraints that make us struggle harder to realize our aims and goals. Sometimes conditions make it almost impossible. But even those who work in more ideal situations have to work within some limits. Successful teaching never happens by itself. It requires a pattern of persistent engagement and effort. No teacher can force a student to learn. Teaching remains a challenge, and its results are uncertain regardless of where it occurs. At a deep level, teaching is no easier for one who works in an "ideal" situation than it is for one working in a disadvantaged setting.

The fact that imagination and energy have a value not determined by outside resources and support gives us hope. By themselves, they are meaningless: One must know what to do with them. This brings us back to the person of the teacher. The power (quality) of the teacher is at the core of the teaching vocation. While circumstances have an enormous impact on teaching, the person of the teacher matters more.

This is not meant to be a naive assertion. Present-day conditions generate deep anxieties and uncertainties. Contradictions continue to multiply between what we say the schools must do and what parents understand education to be, especially for families who feel powerless because of poverty and change over which they have no control. There are students who are afraid of the obstacles that result from injustices. The realities of race, class and ethnicity must be recognized and honored along with the necessity of extensive social and economic restructuring. We cannot fantasize away joblessness, homelessness, disease. Maxine Greene suggests that to call for imaginative capacity is to work for the ability to look at things as if they could be otherwise.[11] When we design our teaching to bring about concentrated awareness, each student's reality must be understood to be interpreted experience. The manner of interpretation depends upon each one's situation and circumstances. It depends upon how many different perspectives a student is able to take. These different perspectives will disclose various aspects of the world. To tap into imagination is to become able to break with what seems fixed and finished. It is to see beyond the given to map out new possibilities. It is hoped that a person may become freed to glimpse what might be and to form ideas of what should be and what is not yet. And all of this while remaining in touch with what apparently *is*.

Sensing the Heart of Things

The role of the imagination is not to resolve, not to point the way, not to improve. It is to awaken, to disclose the ordinarily unseen, unheard and unexpected. But how to feed the imagination? With the arts. The arts awaken imagination. The arts, as Denis Donoghue says, are on the margin, "and the margin is the place for those feelings and intuitions which daily life doesn't have a place for and mostly seems to suppress....With the arts, people can make a space for themselves and fill it with intimations of freedom and presence."[12] We can have our students *participate in the arts* by making and doing things. We can provide occasions for our students *to be enriched by the art of others*. Art enhances imagination because it is evocative.

When we plan our lessons, we are concerned that the class experience will be relevant to the students. Imagination allows us to particularize, to see and hear things in their concreteness in the world. In major languages, the roots of the word *imagination* hint at its play in the world. The Indo-European word means anything changing or intermittent, capable of catching and fixing one's attention. The Sanskrit word means the ever-changing, ensnaring play of appearances. In German, imagination is deceit, something fleeting like a cloud. In Latin, the word means to sparkle, and in Russian imagination is what winks and signals. Imagination is concerned with the changing, spellbinding, arresting, elusive and shimmering. Wallace

Stevens has said, "As in images we awake....It is, we are." "Image," he says, "is an essential poem at the heart of things." Imagination is the sensing of the heart of things.[13]

Through the heart new perspectives open up, new alternatives are recognized, new connections are noticed and the world becomes newly enlightened. Imagination gives us new lenses through which to look at our teaching and to be refreshed. Every now and then, we get glimpses of how imaginative explorations pay off. Sylvia Ashton-Warner describes one such moment that occurred when she began playing "Hark, Hark, the Lark!" on the piano. She speaks of it as the highest peak of achievement in her teaching:

> Whether it was the genius of Schubert speaking over the century through his inspired music, whether it was what I myself felt as I interpreted his music, whether it was the spring in the air after the unprecedentedly cold winter or whether it was ripe to come anyway, it came. There was a flash of yellow to my right; I looked round. It was Twinnie dancing. I thrilled violently. It was not hula or any native dance. It was a fine, exquisite expressive dance, such as is cultivated these days as something new but which belongs to the days before time. It was perfectly in rhythm with the music and followed the feeling of it. Up floated the other Twinnie. They danced to each other, from each other, their arms expressing, their hands and their small bodies. Two small brown spirits with bright yellow jerseys like jonquils....Ronald got up and Matawhere, the little Tamati girls, Riti and Hine, and there was the loveliest sight I have ever seen. Swaying, dipping, whirling to the spring music of Schubert. They had never heard this music before. They had never danced in that wonderful way. It was purely spontaneous....I give all the flowers to Schubert. But I keep one myself for a crown....[14]

It has taken a while, but I have had similar experiences with graduate students. Can you recognize such beautiful, spontaneous bursts of creative engagement from your students? I hope so. I believe so. Let's keep a flower of delight for ourselves!

Reflections: Teaching from Your Heart

Some things to think about from EXPERIENCE:

Over the years, I have developed a course designed to help students better employ the arts in their own teaching. The title of the course may vary slightly in different institutions and settings, but the description is basically the same:

> The Power and Possibilities of Aesthetic Experience to Educate the Whole Person: A wide range of artistic processes such as storytelling, drama and movement will demonstrate how the religious education of people of all age levels can be enhanced.

Here is an excerpt from an essay written by a graduate student in one of the classes:

> I know a man with no imagination, although he considers himself possessed of great imaginative perception. He likes to think, for instance, that there is life on other planets and that these life forms have visited earth and have left their marks for us to ponder and admire, artifacts such as the pyramids. But he thinks this not because he envisions a possibility but because he believes there is proof of it. He believes it is reasonable. And he prides himself on being a realist. He is pleased to call himself a cynic, which to him is the same thing. (He will not vote because all politicians are crooked, all government is corrupt, every cop is on the take.) It satisfies him that he never forgets a wrong. He says, "I forgive, but I don't forget." I do not know, then, what he means by *forgiveness,* for he

nurtures his grudges lovingly and will not disregard their influence. He claims he has been greatly hurt, and now he knows better. I do not deny him his pain, but he has no imagination, so he cannot know better. He will never be wise.

But he is a man of intelligence. (Though he lacks formal education and appears to have what would now be termed "attention deficit disorder." He has never read a book—he claims he cannot concentrate.) He used to read through several newspapers daily so that he could see more than one viewpoint. Now he watches as much educational TV as cable will allow. But nothing effects any changes in him. Intelligence may allow information to become knowledge, but knowledge alone does not necessarily reveal the truth (it can often obscure it) nor does it wield any power over the intellect. It becomes like inert gas passing through an organism and noisily out again. Nothing is really changed. And so he remains, this man, without the imagination necessary for knowledge to evolve into wisdom, rooted in place. Unchanged by the knowledge he has acquired, his gaze never shifts and he sees from one angle only, that from which he stands. His view has long become frozen in time and his interior world informed solely by a vista that has vanished. The career of the human race has progressed, propelled by new experiences—both the good and the ill. New images, information and new knowledge have shaped and changed our anthropology. We adjust and readjust our understanding of the past accordingly, even as we rearrange our plans. But not for him. The world remains fixed in his mind. He is mired in old regrets and old hatred, and he mourns the old sentiments which have been replaced.

He is my father, and I fear for his soul.

—A graduate student

- Do you recognize this person?
- Have you met people like him on your staff or in your classroom?
- Can you relate any ideas from this chapter to the description of the student's father?
- Do you believe there is hope for the father to release his imagination? Why?
- Any suggestions for the graduate student?

St. Gregory of Nyssa said,

> Concepts create idols; only wonder understands anything.

- What do you think he meant?
- Do you see any connection between this statement and the story of the student's father?

Some things to think about from the SCRIPTURES:

Think of what Northrup Frye meant when he wrote,

> The fundamental job of the imagination in ordinary life is to produce out of the society we all have to live in a vision of the society we all want to live in.[15]

Can you relate his words to those in Scripture:

> In the days to come—it is the Lord who speaks
> I will pour out my spirit on all mankind
> Their sons and daughters shall prophesy,
> your young men shall see visions,
> your old men shall dream dreams.
>
> (Acts 2:17 JB)

- How important is it to you to help your students dream dreams?

Praying about Teaching:

Here are two prayers for releasing the imagination. By meditatively reading and praying them, you can make them your own.

> i thank You God for most this amazing
> day:for the leaping greenly spirits of trees
> and a blue true dream of sky;and for everything
> which is natural which is infinite which is yes
>
> (i who have died am alive again today,
> and this is the sun's birthday;this is the birth
> day of life and of love and wings:and of the gay
> great happening illimitably earth)
>
> how should tasting touching hearing seeing
> breathing any—lifted from the no
> of all nothing—human merely being
> doubt unimaginable You?
>
> (now the ears of my ears awake and
> now the eyes of my eyes are opened).[16]
> —E. E. Cummings

And from the Psalms:

> Alleluia!
> I will thank you, Yahweh, with all my heart....
> Great are your works
> to be pondered by all who love them.
> Glorious and sublime are your works;
> your justice stands firm forever.
> You help us to remember your wonders.
> You are compassion and love.
> (Ps 111:1–4)

CHAPTER 4

Teaching Wisely:
Knowing How

The old saying is more true than ever:
any teacher who can be replaced by a machine
(or a book) should be.[1]

—Gabriel Moran

As teachers, we are called to be more than mere dispensers of information. Who among us has not been concerned with "covering the material"? We are an information-loaded society. The idea of loading information into minds regarded as memory banks has too often dominated educational practice. In the last thirty years, there have been several critics of this theory of education. Ivan Illich was the first to shake foundations with the publication of his book, *Deschooling Society.* He called for teachers to reclaim their role of personal teaching and to assume responsibility for the result. He urged them to abandon the merely mechanical process of passing on data and information in an impersonal way to passive students. A few years later, Paulo Freire echoed this refrain. Education, claims Freire, crushes the individual when teachers impose upon the student formulas to memorize and prescriptions to follow. Students are maneuvered and manipulated when they are expected to accept uncritically the information given them. While Freire initially meant his writings for audiences in Brazil, he soon became popular in North America. Teachers sensed that he was on to something when he claimed that "education is an act of love, an act of courage," which should not be reduced to the mere dictation of ideals or the offering of formulas to be stored. Instead, schools should offer students the means of authentic thought and allow them to take in the truth inwardly and not simply superficially.

It is easy to understand why these ideas caught hold, especially among teachers who were becoming more exasperated with trying "to cover the material." It is also easy to understand why some took these ideas to the extreme of "throwing the baby out with the bathwater." Teachers more interested in self-expression or creativity, for example, disregarded rules of grammar, spelling and sentence construction. Many more examples could be cited. Now we have come to realize that information sharing has its place in the teaching process. But we also realize that we can never know all of the information associated with our grade level or subject. There is simply too much for one person, or team of persons, to know. In an age of computers and data banks, web sites and search engines, we realize that more is required of us as teachers than simply to "master the material." We are more aware of the importance of *style*.

Knowing about Knowing

It's not what you say, but how you say it. Kierkegaard insists that teaching is not a question of making true utterances but of uttering the truth in such a way that students want to embrace it.[2] No amount of technique can equal style. Style is more about honesty than it is about charism. If we think we know all the answers, or if we feel we should, we cannot be participants with the students in the learning process. When we withdraw into an attitude of omnipotence, we lose opportunities to learn from our students, and we fail to provide an atmosphere for them to discover what they know. There is a delicate balance between using the appropriate technique to teach something and respecting the needs and responses of students.

> Every life is a point of view directed upon the universe. Strictly speaking, what one life sees no other can...reality happens to be, like a landscape, possessed of an infinite number of perspectives, all equally veracious and authentic. The sole false perspective is that which claims to be the only one there is.[3]
>
> —Jose Ortega y Gasset

If our style of teaching includes the exercise of imagination, our students and we can come to realize that "there is always more to experience, and more in what we experience than we can predict."[4] Explaining and attempting to help students form belief systems and enabling them to come to know are all phases of the teaching activity for any subject matter and any grade level. Such style is focused on transformation of outlook, clearing up a clouded horizon, recognition of relationships. It is evident in the way we handle a complicated question or obstacle, in the way we speak about the material we are presenting, in the way we move from task to task, in short, in the way we are.

A teacher's calling is to be reverently thankful in the presence of information, "material" and technical equipment, and ever humble, critical and tentative about their usefulness in the broader educational goal we share with our students: the enhancement of life. If we can convey to our students some sense of the wonder of existence, we can evoke in them their own longing to give thanks for the gift of life. This is more about style than it is about technique.

If teaching is more than covering the material, what does this suggest about knowing? Here are some conclusions we can draw that have implications for teaching.

First, ordinary consciousness comprises but a small portion of the total activity of the human mind. There is an immense amount of evidence suggesting that unconscious processes make up by far the greater portion of mental activity. These include intuition, creative imagination, spiritual awareness and dreams, to mention a few. This shows that the power of attitudes, beliefs, suggestion, expectation and imagining greatly influence perception, behavior and health.

Unconscious knowing has been demonstrated to be a more pervasive aspect of human experience than we had thought. Biofeedback, hypnotic suggestion and holistic healing continue to inform our theories of knowledge. Individual and cultural beliefs about potentialities greatly affect actual *human potential*. Human potentiality is far greater than is ordinarily realized. Studies of awareness, imagination, empathic understanding, creativity, altruistic love, for example, support this statement.

The mind is not the brain. The mind is not limited in ways implied by models of the physical brain. The correspondence between states of consciousness and human experience is only partial.

The potentialities of creative/intuitive problem solving and choice guidance are far greater than is ordinarily assumed. We all experience this when we "go with our gut feeling," or when we defy logic and choose to follow our heart. All of this means that there are many different ways of knowing.

Teaching for Knowing

We don't exist unless we are deeply and
sensually in touch
with that which can be touched but not known.[5]
—D. H. Lawrence

How do we teach in a way that fosters learning of the
heart? How do we overcome resistance in order to release
imagination, open greater capacities, set free inventiveness
and welcome surprise? It is not easy being faithful to a calling that seeks to honor different ways of knowing. We are
teachers in public space where there are expectations and
pressures. We are involved with students, colleagues, administrators and parents wherever we work. We cannot work
alone; we cannot avoid the social structures beyond our
classroom. We are always negotiating between those structures and our students. This means that we are called to help
students reflect and choose how to live; to sensitize them to
inhumanity and injustice; to understand the ideals of freedom, equality, and respect for self, others and the earth.
These are norms of what *ought to be* in the world we know.
This places burdens on us to constantly reinterpret and make
sense of our own lives.

If we concentrate more on enriching imagination, greater
empathy for the *other* is possible. Imagination makes empathy possible. Of all our cognitive capacities, imagination is
the one that helps us to look through the eyes of others and
hear through their ears. We can break away from the taken-
for-granted, the familiar, and believe in alternative realities
and possibilities. Experiences with works of art can be helpful here in at least two ways. *First,* art can involve us (teacher
and student) with the meaning of human existence in a manner that mere description cannot achieve. *Second,* experiences with the arts offer possibilities for self-confrontation

and self-identification. These experiences can open up new perspectives on what it is to learn and what it is to see.

Paintings, poetry, music, sculpture, dance all engage us by calling on us to wonder, question and feel a wide range of meanings. That is why art is integral to teaching for deeper knowing. Art is not a frill or an "elective," even though many still regard it so. We learn more deeply through that which art evokes in us, by how it enriches the palette of our experience and from the participation it requires of us.

When we teach from the perspective of art, we are more easily inclined to imaginatively reconceive everyday reality and to convey that possibility to the young. If we can see ourselves as on a journey, en route to a place of new openings, then we will be better able to awaken in the young a desire to probe their own worlds and to make sense of them. Of course, these encounters with art—paintings, film, poetry, literature, music—are not meant to be substitutes for the other real worlds like children and old people suffering from war, people suffering from poverty, everyday objects bathed in sunlight or landscapes of faraway places. Encounters with works of art help us not to take these realities for granted. They elicit shock, adventure, exploration, wonder. They are life-enhancing because they evoke more active participation in the quest for deeper and fuller life.

Making Space for Knowing

We experience space in many ways. It feels different to be in an open field than it does to be in a crowded bus. Physical space affects our mental and spiritual space. Open space feels better than crowded space. We can breathe better, think better and move better.

Crowded spaces cause us to feel more tense and constricted. There is also the space of having time to do what we enjoy doing and the lack of space that comes from the pressure of deadlines or the kind of work we must do when we would rather do something else.

It is helpful to reflect on these notions when we design our spaces for teaching. They go beyond the characteristics of physical space. How we organize and present information and the attitude we have toward the responses of our students affect the quality of learning space. It is more effective and gratifying to learn in an environment where the teacher not only speaks but listens, not only gives information but asks questions and welcomes the comments and insights of the students, and encourages students to think for themselves and to help each other learn. Such positive learning space is a powerful tool in teaching. When we use specific methods to create space for learning, we respect our students' capacity for deep knowing. Three features characterize a healthy learning space: *openness, boundaries and hospitality.*[6]

Openness includes an attitude of humility. It means the teacher is open to receive the questions, comments and insights of the students, and the students are comfortable with offering them. It includes a willingness to keep ourselves focused on what is important and not on the trivial. This pertains to the physical space of our classrooms as well. Keeping the room free from clutter conveys a sense of comfort and allows our students to move about with ease, and enables them to move through ideas as well as the material stuff of the classroom more easily.

Boundaries define the learning space. They help us to name the classroom as a focused and privileged place of learning. It takes great care to keep the boundaries clear and apparent. Boundaries help us to teach students which actions are acceptable within these borders and which are not tolerated. Respect for each other, tone of voice, listening skills and appropriate social behaviors are learned and practiced within the classroom boundaries.

Hospitality is the feature that is easiest to recognize—and to miss. It means a warm environment of welcome and acceptance. In teaching, it means creating an atmosphere that says, "I am glad you are here; we are glad you are part of this group." Students can sense whether they are genuinely accepted or just being tolerated. When hospitality is offered authentically, a student is able to say, "I am glad to be here," and really mean it. This sense of hospitality is not a superficial acceptance that glosses over differences. It is born out of a deep commitment to the search for truth that allows us to engage in deep conversations with one another. Good conversations, deep conversations can excite, disturb, discipline or comfort, but they always stimulate inquiry. Good questions initiate learning and are infinitely generative:

> A good question is never answered.
> It is not a bolt to be tightened into place.
> But a seed to be planted and to bear more seed.
> Toward the hope of greening the landscape of ideas.[7]
> —John Ciardi

Therefore, questions require tolerance, respect and honesty. In a hospitable environment, we all can be who we really are; there is no need to pretend or to gloss over differences.

Where hospitality generates deep conversations and good questions, young people may be helped to build bridges among themselves. When we teachers create spaces where this can happen, we are teaching wisely—and we "know" it.

Reflections: Teaching from Your Heart

Some things to think about from EXPERIENCE:

An Arab proverb says,

> God gave us two ears and one mouth to show us that
> we should listen twice as much as we speak.

Teaching and learning require more than speaking. For
many of us, it takes a great deal of reflection to realize that
we often talk too much. It seems that the less prepared or
less confident we are, the more we talk. Maybe this is so
because when we talk, we hear our own voice, and it seems
that we are doing something. But listening is also doing
something.

- Do you agree?
- Have you ever caught yourself talking too much? How
  does it make you feel?
- Can you tolerate silence?
- Are you convinced that you know more than you can
  ever say? What about your students?

How often do you get glimpses of mystery when you
teach? Can you resonate with any of the following?

> You say I am repeating
> Something I have said before. I shall say it again.
> Shall I say it again? In order to arrive there,
> To arrive where you are, to get from where you are not,
> You must go by a way wherein there is no ecstasy.
> In order to arrive at what you do not know
> You must go by a way which is the way of ignorance.
> In order to possess what you do not possess
> You must go by the way of dispossession.
> In order to arrive at what you are not

You must go through the way in which you are not.
And what you do not know is the only thing you know....[8]
—T. S. Eliot

Some things to think about from the SCRIPTURES:

There are many references to wisdom in the Judeo-Christian Scriptures, as a quick glance at a concordance will indicate. One of the most compelling is this:

Those who are wise
will shine like the brightness of the firmament,
and those who turn many to righteousness
like the stars forever and ever.

(Dan 12:3 RSV)

- Does this say anything to you about teachers?
- About yourself?

Praying about Teaching

My heart is full of insight;
I will speak words of wisdom.
(Ps 49:3)

May the spoken words of my mouth,
the thoughts of my heart,
win favor in your sight, O Yahweh.
(Ps 19:14)

CHAPTER 5

Teaching Morally: The Ethic of Caring

We are truly God's work of art,
created in Christ Jesus to live the good life.
(Eph 2:10 JB)

We know from experience that teaching is often lonely, repetitive work that continually asks us to give and leaves us emotionally drained at the end of the day. We cannot avoid thinking: Why do we continue to do it? What keeps us going? The answer is simple but profound: because we *care*. Caring implies fidelity: on the one hand, a state or quality of faithfulness and on the other, a high degree of accuracy. Why *accuracy?* When we are reflectively faithful to someone or something, we try to refine or fine tune our faithfulness. We are in *good faith* when we know what or to whom we are faithful, when we have reflected on the reasons and emotions involved in our faithfulness and when we are committed to fresh affirmations of faithfulness at ever finer and truer levels.[1]

The fidelity we exercise in fulfilling our responsibilities is not just faithfulness to duty or principles, but it is a direct response to our relationship with our students. When we are guided by an ethic of caring, we do not ask whether it is our *duty* to be faithful; rather, faithfulness to persons *is* fidelity. Aristotle describes fidelity in the teacher-learner relationship as a "moral type of friendship, which is not on fixed terms: it makes a gift, or does whatever it does, as to a friend."[2] Further, Aristotle says, we wish that our friends should be good persons, and we wish this for their own sakes. Thus, teaching requires our fidelity to persons. But here is where we need a delicate balance. Fidelity to persons doesn't mean that we compromise standards of academic excellence, the acquisition of skills or accepted norms of behavior. For example, we don't let students "get away with things" because we don't want to offend them. We do not ask how we should treat children so that they will be better able to learn reading or math. Rather, we ask what our teaching of any lesson contributes to the development of good persons. Our guiding principles for reading, math or any other subject are chosen with this ideal in mind. We repeatedly ask ourselves: What effect will this lesson or material have on the person of those I teach? On the wider human community?

But there is even more to it than that. Fidelity goes deeper than questions of method and imagination to qualities of character—our own character. Teachers must have the capacity for eliciting trust as well as the ability to engage in a creative confrontation that is at the heart of all good teaching. This means that we need the personal courage to make demands on our students, to insist that they rewrite a paragraph or report until it makes better sense and to do the work that is necessary to learn well. We need a sense of our own authority.

Authority is both individual and social. We personally earn it, and it is also given to us by the broader community. Authority rests on the legitimate consent of those who willingly render obedience to another in order to accomplish a worthwhile end. But in this authority, students retain their freedom. In other words, when authority is genuine, obedience is freely given.

We probably all have an example of our inability to teach a student who refused to recognize our authority. Perhaps we have some students who have given up on schooling and long for the day when they are done with it. Such students might seem unteachable, and it is easy to give up on them by offering them time-killing exercises or busywork. We do have another choice. We can see these students as persons to whom we have a pedagogical obligation, to whom we owe a good-faith effort. No matter how well we know our material, it is not enough to capture the interest of our students. Nor is it enough to use a creative method of teaching. To be effective, we must have the capacity to engender trust in our authority. Recent ideas on the ethic of caring can be of help to us in trying to achieve that goal.

Spirituality and Caring

The extensiveness of our caring for the well-being of our students is a measure of the richness of our own spirituality. Students bring a host of personal concerns to the classroom, and so do we as teachers. Yet, the burden is on us as teachers to "put off to the side" our own needs, moods and anxieties. Our obligation is to teach—that is, to serve. *We owe our students a good deal more than students owe us.* These moral obligations make teaching an ever-demanding task. So it is not surprising that every teacher will occasionally fall short of her or his own expectations. The wonder is how often most of us are able to meet them.

It helps to think of ourselves as moral beings who are concerned with defining our own life purposes in a way that arouses our students to do the same. The zest for our moral lives that we display to our students has the capacity to stir their hearts and minds. Young people are more likely to be affected by teachers who themselves are questioning, pondering and learning.

Obviously, this process differs for various age levels. Young people have to pass through stages of development to be able to think about what they are doing and to take responsibility. We can recognize three aspects of our task:

1. Equipping young people with the ability to identify alternatives and to see results and possibilities in the situations they confront;
2. Teaching principles and perspectives by means of which those situations can be evaluated, as well as the norms that should guide their choices;
3. Enabling students to make decisions of principle; to reflect, to articulate and to act in good faith.

A sense of moral "oughtness" is essential to this whole process. Along with a sense of self, there must be attentiveness to others. A rich imagination is needed to discover ways of living together justly and pursuing common goals. None of this will happen unless we as teachers are committed to looking through the eyes of each of our students and confronting the lived reality and possibility of the common good of all of us. It will help us if we can give our students splendid and striking examples of those who live virtuous lives.

Teaching for Virtue

Virtue can be caught and taught.[3]
—Thomas Lickona

We now recognize this to be true. In the 1970s education began a phase of values clarification in which the slogan was, "Values are caught not taught." One of its principles was that the teacher should never directly tell students what is right or wrong; instead, students should be left to discover "values" on their own. Many teachers now recognize that failing to do their job of inculcating moral principles exacts a price that is paid by bewildered students who are being denied a structured way to develop values. The result is moral relativism. Students deserve better.

How sad it is that many teachers feel unable to defend their own beliefs—for example, that cheating is wrong. Those of us who teach in religious schools should be able to declare that there really is such a thing as moral knowledge and that our religious tradition has something to say about it. We have learned something about basic decency, about human rights and vice and virtue, over several thousand years of civilization. This knowledge is preserved in our religious inheritance: the teachings, traditions and lives of the people who share our common story.

Throughout history, moral education was accomplished using moral tales and parables. Saul Bellow maintains that the survival of Jewish culture would be inconceivable without the stories that gave meaning to the Jewish moral tradition. One such story is called "If Not Higher." It can help to make the point.

> There was once a rabbi in a small Jewish village in Russia who vanished every Friday morning for several hours. The devoted villagers boasted that during these hours their rabbi ascended to Heaven to talk with God. A skeptical newcomer arrived in town, determined to discover where the rabbi really was.
>
> One Friday morning the newcomer hid near the rabbi's house, watched him rise, say his prayers and put on the clothes of a peasant. He saw him take an ax and go into the forest, chop down a tree and gather a large bundle of wood. Next, the rabbi proceeded to a shack

in the poorest section of the village in which lived an old woman and her sick son. He left them the wood, which was enough for the week. The rabbi then quietly returned to his own house.

The story concludes that the newcomer stayed on in the village and became a disciple of the rabbi. And whenever he hears one of his fellow villagers say, "On Friday morning our rabbi ascends all the way to Heaven," the newcomer quietly adds, "If not higher."[4]

This story is unlike the sterile moral dilemmas of value clarification in which there is no obvious right and wrong, no clear virtue and vice. The dilemmas may engage the minds of the students, but they only marginally engage their emotions. It is difficult to get students to "care" about the characters. And it is hard to imagine parents and teachers imparting the moral dilemmas of seven people in a lifeboat with provisions for only four in the scenario commonly used in values clarification exercises.

In contrast, in the story of the rabbi and the skeptical outsider it is not up to the listener to decide whether the rabbi did the right thing. The moral message is clear: "Here is a good man—merciful, compassionate and helpful to the weak and vulnerable. *Be like that person.*" The message is contagious. Even the skeptic gets the point.[5]

Of course, stories and parables are not always appropriate for high school or college ethics courses, but the literary classics certainly are. So are Bible stories. Students can be helped to understand and sympathize with what the author is saying about the moral ties that bind the characters and hold in place the social fabric in which they play their roles. As teachers we must care enough to help our students become acquainted with their moral heritage in religion, literature and philosophy. An agreeable atmosphere will enhance our caring. Such an atmosphere is one in which

- there will be behavior codes that emphasize civility, kindness and honesty;
- teachers will be praised and rewarded for insisting on basic respect, decency, honesty and fairness;
- children will be told stories that reinforce goodness; in high school and college, students will be reading, studying and discussing the moral classics.

To sum up, virtue can be taught *and* caught. To teach morally is to help make students keenly aware that their *own character* is at stake.

Teaching as Caring

No matter which grade level we teach, we are called on to be sources of moral counsel. We must routinely put our own integrity and sense of judgment on public display. There is no escape from this. It makes claims on us. We could say that we have an obligation to try to realize the ideals we express in ourselves and others. We begin to realize that if we are to expect our students to understand moral rules and principles, this will include being a certain kind of person ourselves.

Helping students respond to issues and situations can be unsettling. We find ourselves asking—while students look on—"How should I react? What is the right thing to say? What should I do?" It doesn't take long to realize that students at every level of education seem to tune in closely at such moments. Even a teacher who refuses to offer a response is sending a signal to the students—namely that she or he has no intellectual or moral stance on the subject and would rather "pass the buck." But we cannot do this.

Teaching is always and at once both an intellectual and a moral endeavor. The two aspects are thoroughly intertwined. We may have had conversations with those who try to argue that the fundamental purpose of education is to teach the mind. But in the concrete circumstances of learning and living in schools, the mind becomes much more than a cognitive object. The mind becomes an evolving constellation of attitudes, dispositions and capacities that takes shape through the process of education.[6]

Think about it. A math teacher might claim to teach students only to think well in the manipulation of numbers. But "thinking well" involves self-discipline, concentration, effort, imagination and more, all of which extend beyond doing math to how one addresses the questions that arise in life. To claim that one is "only" teaching good thinking or good understanding of subject matter presupposes a moral conviction that *a student's life will be better because of that teaching*. Otherwise, why engage in it?

Our understanding of teaching as a vocation helps us to draw these dimensions together. Teachers who deal with "neutral" subject matter (chemistry, earth science, reading, for example) have, at some level, the conviction that it is better for a student to know the material than never to be exposed to it. They feel that they are enabling students to move from a less desirable to a better position through their teaching. In fact, the concept of teaching implies that there is something worthwhile to attain. What is this *something*? It is the stretching and expanding of the students' world and the nurturing of the students' ethical ideal. This is what makes the activity worth the effort. The teacher *cares*.

A teacher cannot preach this ethic of caring. She or he must live it. That implies establishing a relationship with the students, besides talking to them and showing them care. In addition, he or she teaches all subjects with emphasis on their social and personal aspects, showing how human beings are affected by them and pointing out the responsibilities that flow from them.

Everything we do as teachers has moral implications. Through *dialogue, modeling, practice and the assignment of best motive,* a caring teacher nurtures the ethical ideal.[7] What we reflect to our students contributes to the enhancement of that ideal if we meet our students as they are and find something admirable in them. As a result of this *confirmation,* our students may find the strength to become even more admirable. We leave them with an image that is lovelier than the one they had of themselves. We do not need to establish a deep, lasting, time-consuming personal relationship with every student. What we must do is to be present to each student as she or he addresses us.

In sum, to teach morally, we need to care.

Reflections: Teaching from Your Heart

Some things to think about from EXPERIENCE:

> Treat people as if they were what they ought to be and you help them become what they are capable of being.
> —Johann Wolfgang von Goethe

No doubt, you have heard of the Pygmalion effect and probably experienced it many times. The psychological phenomenon of which we had been instinctively aware has now been scientifically documented. People conform to the image of them that we project. Working with classes of children with comparable backgrounds and IQs, Robert Rosenthal established that students embody their teachers' ideals of them.

- Can you recall a specific example from your own teaching experience?
- How might this example influence your teaching?
- How about yourself—have you had a teacher believe in you in this way?

John Ruskin wrote:

> The entire object of true education
> is to make people not merely to do the right things
> but to enjoy them;
> not merely industrious,
> but to love industry;
> not merely learned;
> but to love knowledge;
> not merely pure;
> but to love purity;
> not merely just,
> but to hunger and thirst
> after justice.[8]

- How can you relate these words to the challenge of teaching morally?
- Would you add anything to the above?

Something to think about from the SCRIPTURES:

Think of how the following passage relates to your teaching:

> You are the light of the world. A city built on a hill-top cannot be hidden. No one lights a lamp to put it under a tub; they put it on the lamp-stand where it shines for everyone in the house. In the same way your light must shine in the sight of [all], so that seeing your good works, they may give the praise to your Father in heaven.
> (Matt 5:14–16 NJB)

- Do you see any connection between this Scripture passage and the following paragraph from this chapter?

No matter which grade level we teach, we are called on to be sources of moral counsel. We must routinely put our own integrity and our sense of judgment on public display. There is no escape from this. It makes claims on us. We could say that we have an obligation to try to realize the ideals we express in ourselves and others. We begin to realize that if we are to expect our students to understand moral rules and principles, this will include "being a certain kind of person ourselves."

Praying about Teaching:

Perhaps the words of either of these two poets can inspire your prayer:

> With God to help me I will stand firm.
> (Ps 56: 4)

Or,

> Blessed sister, holy mother, spirit of the fountain,
> Spirit of the garden,
> Suffer us not to mock ourselves with falsehood
> Teach us to care and not to care
> Teach us to sit still
> Even among these rocks.
> Our peace in His will
> And even among these rocks...
> Let my cry come unto Thee.[9]
>
> —T. S. Eliot

CHAPTER 6

Facing Ourselves
Facing the Unfamiliar:
Multiple Vulnerabilities

If only I had the confidence of being a good teacher. But I'm not even an appalling teacher. I don't even claim to be a teacher at all. I'm just a nitwit somehow let loose among children.[1]

—Sylvia Ashton-Warner

How many of us have secretly felt this way while we are pressed to continue our work! Moments of self-doubt find their way into our lives whether we teach five-year-olds or thirty-five-year-olds. We try to think of reasons for them, as did Sylvia Ashton-Warner:

If only I kept workbooks and made schemes and taught like other teachers, I should have the confidence of numbers. It's the payment, the price of walking alone.

Yet...I've got to do what I believe. And I believe in all I do. It's this price one continually pays for stepping out of line. I'm feeling too old to pay it.

But I must do what I believe in or nothing at all.[2]

This is every teacher's dilemma. In spite of all our education and experience, we are still very vulnerable. It often doesn't take much to remind us of just how vulnerable we really are. As teachers, we are dedicated to pursue the worthwhile. Just what is worthwhile is largely defined in the day-to-day life of the classroom. We have to be concerned with specific actions and actual decisions, not those found in textbooks we studied in teacher preparation classes.

Our concern is with *this* class and *these* students. As we prepare our lessons, we have to decide what to do in order to focus on worthwhile achievement. We have to decide how to communicate information, when to permit free, creative activity in place of required tasks, whether to nurture sensitivity in certain situations instead of encouraging cognitive actions. Ashton-Warner was constantly dealing with these *multiple small uncertainties,* as the above passages reveal. We face these almost every day—or *at least we should*—whom should we call on, whom to discipline, whom to reward, whether to pay attention to the rhythms of the students' inner time or to follow the clock, etcetera. When we consider our choices, we feel that we must justify them to persuade ourselves and others that we are doing what is right.

So much of what we do is precarious. Even in the best circumstances, we are faced with predicaments. Teachers must establish some control while motivating students and ensuring that they actually learn. We must insist that our students do tasks that are sometimes boring and often difficult. Frequently, their emotional demands drain us, and sometimes our inability to meet all of their intellectual needs frustrates us. And there are wider uncertainties. In the last twenty years or so, teachers have suffered a loss of social esteem and status. Parents are more critical, demanding and divided. It is more difficult to establish a common set of expectations that support our efforts to maintain discipline and inspire our students. We sometimes feel alone.

Teaching has never been easy. Like parenting, one can never be fully prepared for all of the demands of teaching. The loftier our goals, the more likely we are to fail to measure up to them. Yet we continue, despite the drain:

> Back to school after two snow days—good to be back although I have a slight flu. Mary looking tired from weeks of strep and family turmoil.
>
> Ronnie, with bad cough and sore throat and looking feverish, pulled me close to him and said his parents went to court to fight over who should care for him.
>
> Annie was full of anxious chatter about moving to a new house in a few weeks.
>
> Carol brings a Haitian friend who speaks no English to visit for the day.
>
> Joey's mother weeps from homesickness for Taiwan. Debbie nervously admits that she left her notebooks at home. All this between 8:30 and 8:45 A.M.
>
> —Elementary school teacher's journal

> 7:45 A.M. Feeling partially liberated. How can anyone claim to "love" teaching if he feels such relief when it's over and done? Two more classes, easy ones, ahead, then months and months, perhaps eighteen months, without classes. What bliss in prospect. Yet I don't feel like retiring completely yet.
>
> But why does a class like yesterday's, the final class, seem so scary in prospect, so difficult in execution? It was not very good, truth is, because I was tense and pushing—telling them rather than teaching them.
>
> —College teacher's journal

Sound familiar? As reported in research on teachers, diaries of teachers are filled with references to all the students they have failed to serve or reach. In these private reflections, teachers are also torn between the way they would prefer to teach and the demands of prescribed curricula.[3] Does this sound like burnout? It could. But I agree with the author of the second journal entry who also wrote "it sounds more like evidence that this profession can never become boring. If I get bored *here,* it is my fault, not the fault of anything in teaching."

Teaching is unpredictable from hour to hour, from minute to minute. There are tears when you don't expect them, laughter when you might predict tears. There are flashes of insight and embarrassing displays of ignorance. The results are usually uncertain. And here's the rub: The more attuned we are to the needs of our students, the more unsure we are of what they or we actually achieve. While we guide, stimulate and challenge, at the same time we must feel the most tender regard for each student's privacy and being. What is a teacher to do? A good place to begin is by talking to other teachers. If we want to grow as teachers, we must learn to talk to one another about our inner lives—about our own identity and integrity.

Schools can be places where teachers come together to live out their vocation, not only places to engage in activities in order to satisfy accrediting agencies. I believe it is possible for schools to be forums of learning that are shaped to help teachers view their work as participation in the formation of another's story and to have their own story influenced by the other. Such a vocation is to answer the call of the *community* and *tradition.* The *community* includes the youth, adults and families served by the school. The *traditions* are the communal recollections and hope that give structure, meaning and value to individual and collective life.[4]

Facing Ourselves, Together

...when you come to think about it, you find that of the two lands of order, the conscious and the unconscious order, only one is real. It's the order in the deep hidden places....The true order in the depths. The "still centre."[5]
—Sylvia Ashton-Warner

The call to teach is embedded in mystery. The more we engage with our students as persons, the more we affirm our own incompleteness. We become more aware of spaces still to be explored, desires still to be uncovered, possibilities still to be opened. For many of us, our sense of incompleteness is heightened by *how we handle our time and our vulnerability.*

Time. Soon after we first answer our calling to be teachers, we are confronted with the dilemma of how to spend our time. Some of us have learned to hoard time as a miser hoards money. There just never seems to be enough time to do what needs to be done. We are faced with making priorities for ourselves: family responsibilities, personal needs, demands of friendship, professional tasks. Some of us feel the pressure to carefully account for every moment. Is it all right to splurge now and then to spend an afternoon with friends? To take time out to play with our own children? To try out some new recipes? To read a novel or see a play? Those who are time hoarders will recognize these dilemmas. Always lurking in the backs of our minds is the concern about keeping up with our fields of teaching. We may feel forever behind with trying to keep up with professional reading or attending workshops and seminars, and therefore think of ourselves as failing in our duty. There is just so much to do.

Vulnerability. No matter what age group we teach, we are always "on," always exposed to others. We are scrutinized and judged daily by all the students we teach. This can be very draining. We can grow weary of performing, entertaining, stimulating and filling up others' emptiness. We can tire of trying to stimulate, encourage, comfort and discipline our students. But if we open our hearts to the wisdom of experience, we can have fewer such days. We can come to realize that students must learn and achieve for themselves, not to please their teachers. There will always be those who do not meet our standards, and it takes quite a bit of humility to admit this. Our concern for our students does not excuse us from the obligation to exercise our authority, evaluate student progress and attend to the standards set by the broader community, as well as nurture students in an atmosphere of warmth and understanding. By so doing, teachers rediscover the value of care. We reach back to our own experiences of caring and being cared for, and as Nel Noddings writes, we embrace the ideal of nurture through "dialogue, practice and confirmation."[6] How does this process look?

Dialogue is difficult because it requires rethinking our notion of authority. It does not mean that we surrender it. The teacher cannot pretend to be the same as the student. The teacher is the one who is responsible for designing the environment to make teaching and learning possible. Dialogue requires a conversation between the content or curriculum and the students' needs. It means allowing their problems and questions to deepen within them and then helping them to express them even if it means that some tension might result. We should not forget that tension can be creative.

Practice implies a climate of hospitality in which genuine conversations can take place. Henri Nouwen complained that the classroom is often an inhospitable place, and he calls for the "creation of a space where students can enter into a fearless communication with each other and allow their respective life experiences to be their primary and most valuable source of growth and maturation."[7] Students are allowed to ask questions and to think creatively about the content. Perhaps some of us can recall how it felt when we asked a question that was ignored, or when we were told to put our hand down when we were poised to ask a question. While we as teachers have objectives and goals, the students have needs that must be addressed. The burden is on us to prepare our material as well as possible, deliver it as efficiently and creatively as possible, yet be willing to adjust our methods and materials to the unique setting in which we are teaching. We cannot teach the same way year after year. Recall the joke in the question, "Do you have twenty years of experience, or one year of experience repeated twenty times?" Our practice of teaching requires fresh style.

Confirmation is what results from an environment of hospitality in which dialogue is practiced. It is cyclic. The stronger and more confident students become, the braver they are to take risks and try things they had never had the courage for. They can tap their own resources. It is interesting that as the students are confirmed, so are we as teachers. Confirmation affirms us as persons and teachers. When our students listen to us attentively, give us verbal and nonverbal support or a word of thanks, we are made bolder and we try harder. The song from *The King and I* says it well:

> It's a very old saying
> but it's a true and honest thought
> that if you are a teacher
> by your students you'll be taught.[8]
> —Oscar Hammerstein, "Getting to Know You"
>   (paraphrased)

Facing the Unfamiliar

In spite of all the vulnerabilities we feel in carrying out the day-to-day tasks of teaching, the fact remains that we are engaged in exciting work. This is because we are constantly called upon to deal with the *unfamiliar*. The frontiers of teaching are infinitely broad and expanding. Each time we teach a new course, we embark on a new adventure full of risk and uncertainty that causes us to stretch our talents and abilities. So it is when we teach a new class of students. Truly, our work, our calling, is hardly boring. It continuously puts demands on our soul. Sophie Freud puts it well, "Nothing demands more inner discipline than self-imposed work."[9] It takes work and inner discipline to be creative. We have to be willing to stick with the process, often at the expense of going to a movie, visiting friends or cooking a special meal, for example. We can become exasperated at having to prioritize, especially when we ourselves have chosen this path.

There is also the response of our students. How will they react to this new idea or novel method, to this strange bit of information or unusual work of art? Amidst the novelty, we can discover the depths of our vulnerability. How devastated are we after one student's negative comment? Can it put us off the mark for days? Is there any way to become less vulnerable? Probably not. The more risks we take, the more vulnerable we become. But we can become less devastated by criticism and more able to learn from it. We can reconcile ourselves to the fact that we will never be liked or appreciated by all our students all the time. We can realize that in the process of becoming more open and more vulnerable, we can become stronger.

There is one more vulnerability that can haunt our soul—the fear that comes with success. It creeps up as we are relishing our success after a particularly good day, exhilarating lesson or demonstration. Back in the recesses of our mind, we wonder what we can do for an encore. How will we live up to these new standards or expectations? Will next week's class or tomorrow's lesson be as stimulating? Are the compliments about this class really a subtle criticism of other classes?

What keeps us going? I believe it is *passion for our work*. Yet, although passion for our work makes us less dependent on other people, it does not insure invulnerability.[10] Teaching is fraught with paradoxes. We still need to rely on students, schools and material goods to make teaching possible. Passion alone is not enough. A teacher's calling demands that we embrace the paradoxes inherent in our response:

> ...the paradoxes of my life are related to being a student and teacher of topics that intimately touch my own and other people's lives. Such a field demands total devotion to its subject matter, as well as providing rich and varied life experiences. It demands tight self-discipline and loose creativity. It demands openness to people and absorption with ideas, protection of time and energy, as well as endless commitment to students. It demands both solitude and many human encounters. It demands skills of objectivity, observation and involvement, distance as well as intimacy. It demands self-assurance, power and humility.[11]

Such is the passion that makes us teach amidst so many paradoxes. Who will know if we are adequate to the calling? Thomas More had a glimmer of the answer when in Robert Bolt's play, *A Man for All Seasons,* he suggests to the young Richard,

"Why not be a teacher? You'd be a fine teacher. Perhaps even a great one."

And Richard answers,

"And if I was, who would know it?"

To which More replies,

"You, your pupils, your friends, God. Not a bad public that...."[12]

Indeed.

Reflections: Teaching from Your Heart

Some things to think about from EXPERIENCE:

Here is another true story.

It was her very first week of teaching high school. Somehow, all the girls in her classes seemed big—they were as tall or taller than she was, and some of them even seemed more self-confident. Diane was trying to figure out what was going on inside of her—she felt anxious yet eager. Surely, these are "beginner's jitters," she thought. "It will get better." After the first class, Diane stepped into the corridor to catch her breath before the next one. She noticed Mercedes, who taught in the room across from hers. "The class period goes by too quickly," Mercedes said, as she glanced over at Diane. "I hardly ever manage to cover all that I planned." Just as Diane was about to respond, Mercedes said, "Oops, I better get back in the room before the next group arrives. I have to get some things ready." And she quickly disappeared.

Mercedes was a seasoned teacher of about thirty-five years. She was known for her high standards and competent teaching. She expected a lot of her students—she was strict—and the girls loved her. "Why in the world is she so rushed to get ready for the next class," mused Diane. "It's another class in American History...the same subject she just finished teaching in the previous class period." After dismissal for the day, Diane made a point to approach Mercedes in the student locker room where they both were on duty for the week. "Can I ask you something," Diane asked. "Sure, what can I do for you?" Mercedes replied as they made their way up the stairs. "I was surprised that you seemed so anxious to get back into your classroom this morning when you were just going to meet a class for the same subject you had just finished teaching. Is there something special about that second class?" Mercedes paused for a moment and with a twinkle in her eye said, "Sure, they are a different class...different girls." "Oh," said Diane. There was no need for a further exchange at that moment.

Later that evening as Diane was preparing for the next day's classes, she smiled as she recalled Mercedes' words. She thought to herself, "I guess that's why she is such a good teacher. She is always trying to teach *each* class as best as she can. That takes a lot of work...and a lot of anxiety, too." Diane sighed, and then thought, "I hope I can be as good a teacher as Mercedes is...and I guess there is no shortcut. I'll have to pay the price."

- Does any one of the above sound familiar to you?
- What are some of your own fears in the classroom?
- How have you dealt with them?
- Do you have any fears in relation to your colleagues?
- How have you dealt with them?
- In what ways do you feel vulnerable as a teacher?
- What might you do about these feelings?

The philosopher William James once said,

> The deepest principle in human nature is the craving to be appreciated.

- Do you agree?
- If so, in what ways do you find this to be true of your students? Of yourself?
- Does it help you to be reminded that others worry or are anxious about their teaching?

Perhaps the following has something to say to your heart:

> So here I am, in the middle way, having had twenty
> years—

Twenty years largely wasted...
Trying to learn to use words, and every attempt
Is a wholly new start, and a different kind of failure
Because one has only learnt to get the better of words
For the thing one no longer has to say, or the way in
  which
One is no longer disposed to say it. And so each venture
Is a new beginning, a raid on the inarticulate
With shabby equipment always deteriorating
In the general mess of imprecision of feeling.
Undisciplined squads of emotion. And what there is to
  conquer
By strength and submission, has already been
  discovered
Once or twice, or several times, by men [and women]
  who cannot hope
To emulate—but there is no competition—
There is only the fight to recover what has been lost
And found again and again: and now, under conditions
That seem unpropitious. But perhaps neither gain nor
  loss.
For us, there is only the trying. The rest is not our
  business.[13]

—T. S. Eliot

- Is there a line in the poem that rings especially true for you? Why?
- How are you vulnerable in your teaching?
- What helps you to cope with your vulnerabilities?

Is the following advice helpful?

> Be patient with everyone, but above all with your-self....Do not be disheartened by your imperfections, but always rise up with fresh courage. How are we to be patient in dealing with our neighbor's faults if we are impatient in dealing with our own? They who are fretted

by their own failings will not correct them. All profitable correction comes from a calm and peaceful mind.

—Saint Francis de Sales

- Do you talk about your vulnerabilities with your colleagues? With anyone else?
- Do you think it is beneficial to do so? Why?

Some things to think about from the SCRIPTURES:

Consider this text:

> Do not be anxious about anything, but in everything, by prayer and petition, with thanksgiving, present your requests to God. And the peace of God, which transcends all understanding, will guard your heart and your minds in Christ Jesus.
>
> (Phil 4: 6–7 NIV)

- What can this passage teach you about your feelings toward teaching?
- Do you pray for your students? If so, how regularly?
- Is prayer a part of your lesson preparation?

Praying about Teaching:

> When my heart had been growing sour
> and I was pained in my innermost parts,
> I had been foolish and misunderstood;...
> Nevertheless, I waited in your presence;
> you grasped my right hand.
> Now guide me with your counsel....
>
> (Ps 73:21–24)

CHAPTER 7

The Joy of Teaching:
A Portrait of Possibility

Go after her and seek her;
She will reveal herself to you;
Once you hold her, do not let her go.
For in the end you will find rest in her
And she will take the form of joy for you.
(Sir 6:27–28 NJB)

With these poetic words, the author of the ancient Scripture describes what the gift of wisdom means and shines brilliant beams of light on the path we have been exploring in this book. For teachers, wisdom brings with her a deep sense of the larger purpose we share with others—our common work. This work involves the integration of the spiritual dimension of life with the rest of life at the personal and social levels. It is a grandiose task except for one simple truth: The only way to approach it is through each of us doing our own inner work and working on our relationships with one another.

Søren Kierkegaard suggests that the larger the vision, the more particular and focused the work: "The more sacred the object of your search, the nearer it is to you."[1] To do the common work, we must explore the deepest and most sacred part of our own selves. It requires continually becoming awake and open to deeper levels of our own inner life and intentionally nurturing them if we would do the same for our students.

When we answered the call to become teachers, we were responding to reasons and sensations deep in our souls. Through the years, we continue to discover how best to direct our energy and passion for our work. Sometimes our learning is a confirmation of what we already think and who we already are. But every now and then, we look upon ourselves with self-awareness and notice something new. These are the moments when we have a chance at changing and flourishing. They are moments of profound paradox:

> To arrive where you are, to get from where you are not,
> You must go by a way wherein there is no ecstasy.
> In order to arrive at what you do not know
> You must go by a way which is the way of ignorance.
> In order to possess what you do not possess
> You must go by the way of dispossession.
> In order to arrive at what you are not
> You must go through the way in which you are not
> And what you do not know is the only thing you know
> And what you own is what you do not own
> And where you are is where you are not.
>
> —T. S. Eliot[2]

Can you relate to these paradoxes? Eliot is giving us a timeless description of the path by which truth is realized. It is a path that jostles us continually with its lack of certainty. It is a journey of wonder and "not-knowing."

Teaching as Journeying

The journey of life is full of surprises. Sometimes they are joyful, but at other times we want a little more direction, a little more certainty. We really want to know what our purpose is, especially after a few trying days, so we conclude what we think it is too quickly, and in so doing close ourselves to new ways. This is a real dilemma. How can we live so that we can catch a glimmer of our purpose, while remembering that we alone don't determine it? Can we live out our vocation in such a way as to invite mystery?

> And what you thought you came for
> Is only a shell, a husk of meaning
> From which the purpose breaks only when it is fulfilled
> If at all. Either you had no purpose
> Or the purpose is beyond the end you figured
> And is altered in fulfillment.
>
> —T. S. Eliot[3]

Living out our vocation is both an *inner* and *outer* journey.

An inner journey. As previous chapters of this book tried to show, teaching is more than a classroom activity or even a professional activity. It is a basic human art that depends upon the exercise of certain intellectual, moral and spiritual virtues. To excel requires more than theory and technique. It requires the cultivation of certain moral and spiritual values that are indispensable to learning of any kind anywhere.

This is easy to admit when we ponder the response to a simple question we can put to others. If we say, "Name two or three of the most important teachers in your life," we will be quick to notice that few professionally trained teachers usually make the list. It is more than likely that people will name parents, friends, neighbors, spouses, siblings or other relatives. Then if you ask what each had in common, very few would name technique or style. On the contrary, most will describe certain qualities of character—compassion, integrity, dedication, empathy, truthfulness, attentiveness and love. This simple activity shows that people know good teaching when they experience it, and when they try to describe it, they rarely do so in terms of technique. That is amazing given all the literature that emphasizes technique over almost everything else.

When describing their favorite teachers, people spontaneously connect the vocation of teaching with the arts of moral and spiritual formation more than with academic specialization. Today's students still recognize some of the most ancient wisdom about the vocation of teaching, namely, that teaching is, finally, a spiritual calling. It is only on the basis of a religious account of teaching that its true character can be fully grasped. The religious explanation of teaching strongly insists that virtues like piety, charity, humility and faith are not just virtues that help one to become a good teacher. The connection between moral and spiritual virtues to excellence in teaching is one of interdependence—you can't have one without the other.

Recall the famous work *Meno* by Plato. This was Plato's only dialogue on the subject of education. It features a character whose failure to learn is mostly the result of flaws in his character rather than in his logical ability. Through the main character, Meno, Plato shows us that when a student wishes to learn the truth, he or she must change. To the extent that the truth comes to Meno, he does change. He becomes less arrogant, more self-disciplined and more courageous, not just in his ideas but in his way of living. Moral and spiritual virtues improve thought itself as well as action. The implication is clear: the more we work on our inner life, the better teachers we will be.

And how will our inner journeys affect the learning of our students? Regardless of subject matter, grade level or age group, as we attend to our own inner work we will see that our task is to enable students to work for the kind of human excellence that integrates the moral, spiritual and intellectual dimensions of the virtues. St. Bernard of Clairvaux sums up this religious vision of pedagogy in these words:

> Some seek knowledge for the sake of knowledge:
>   that is curiosity;
> others seek knowledge that they may themselves be
>   known: that is vanity;
> but there are still others who seek knowledge in order
>   to serve and edify others, and that is charity.[4]

An outer journey. The inner work required in teaching leads to an outer journey as well. While inner work is a deeply personal matter, it is not a private matter. We do our work in community, and there are ways to be together in community that can help us with our inner work. *Teaching is a public activity.* As such, it is improved through practice and criticism. We can learn from others. If we really stop and think about it, we probably have learned a great deal about teaching from our conversations with other teachers, from sharing ideas and hints about what worked well and what just didn't fly, and most important, from noticing and observing other teachers at work, if only at random. While teaching is closer to an art than it is to a technique and involves a certain amount of mystery, we as teachers can recognize it, own its effectiveness and embrace its power and its possibilities.

Our inner-outer journey as teachers allows us the great insight that we cocreate the world as we live out our vocations. As Parker Palmer puts it, "we live in and through a complex interaction of spirit and matter, a complex interaction of what is inside us and what is 'out there.' The insight of our spiritual traditions is not to deny the reality of the outer world, but to help us understand that we create that world, in part, by projecting our spirit on it—for better or worse."[5] This is both an awesome responsibility and a source of profound hope for change.

A Portrait of Possibility

As cocreators, we recognize that it doesn't all depend upon us. Perhaps when we were young we believed that ultimate responsibility for successful teaching rested on us alone. As we mature, we learn that we do not carry the whole burden of teaching by ourselves. We share the load with others. Our schools can be places where we can seek out helpful colleagues, confirming administrators and engaged parents. We more readily admit that our vocation as teachers depends upon faith. We more humbly admit that the final fruits of our efforts rest in God's hands. Our failure to teach with such hope will only make our calling become an intolerable and lonely burden. But to have confidence in the promises of the One who calls us sustains us in our common work and helps us to "keep heart" in our calling.

Teaching assumes hope. Even though the act of teaching fully occupies the present moment, its goal is oriented to the future...to the possible. For many teachers, this passion for the possible is what nourishes them and gives them joy. This deep, abiding joy, is the experience that Sartre calls "joy-feeling."[6] In "joy-feeling" we are receptive, addressed, supplied with intention and creativity. As an emotion, "joy-feeling" is delightful and, as basic affect, it helps us to recognize our relatedness to others, self, the world and God. It gives us insight into the deeper meaning and power of what can happen whenever we teach:

> There's nothing so small but I love it and choose
> to paint it gold—groundly and great
> and hold it most precious and know not whose
> soul it may liberate....[7]
> —Rainer Maria Rilke

We never really know what in our teaching will open a door for a student, validate a feeling, expand a horizon, challenge an assumption or release her or his imagination. Sometimes we function as a stranger to our students, not just a companion or guide. Strangers can be spiritual guides who bear truths that tend to shake common perceptions and assumptions. A stranger helps others to see that truth is a large matter that requires various perspectives, restatements of truths and recreation of reality. Seen this way, the process of education involves the encountering of *that which is not me,* of the different, the strange.

Many authors have explored this theme. Parker Palmer, in his book, *The Company of Strangers,* depicts the educational significance of the stranger in our midst.[8] Similarly, Hans Küng, in his book, *The Church,* speaks of the educational importance of the alien in our midst.[9] Anyone who is different than I am poses a question to me. The differences between us are an opening into new possibilities for both of us. In commenting on this dynamic, Dwayne Huebner remarks that differences are invitations to be led out *(educare),* to be educated. But "we cannot recognize the invitation if we look at the other as a mirror image of extension of our own self."[10] One writer clearly expresses this temptation: "Our fundamental anxiety is that we will pass through the world and leave no mark; that anxiety is what induces us to devise projects for ourselves, to live among our fellow beings and reach out to them, to interpret life from situated standpoints to try—over and over again—to begin."[11] But we must overcome any temptation to make our students into mirror images of ourselves; we must recognize and reverence their otherness. We must be content with "leaving thumbprints as we pass."

There is another spiritual insight to be had as we further probe our teacher's calling as a journey: If we see our calling as a quest, we open the way to also seeing our own lives in terms of process and possibilities, in terms of "a route, an experience which gradually clarifies itself, which gradually rectifies itself and proceeds by dialogue with itself and with others."[12] Just as we are artists who make our lives from the materials available, we are also travelers, adventurers, who risk taking the journey of teaching. As we take the time to reflect on our life's journey as a teacher, we come to realize that we have been on an adventure that has enabled each of us, as Maxine Greene puts it, "to look through others' eyes more than I would have and to imagine being something more than I have come to be."[13] All along, while we have been teaching others, we have been feeding our own soul. And all of this happened while answering *a teacher's calling.*

All Our Life Is a Circle

When we ponder and pray over the meaning of our life, we spiral deeper in its mysterious circle. And if we are graced, as I believe we are, we become increasingly aware that the communion we seek is all around us. We understand that deep inside of every student, indeed, of every person, is some sense of wonder of life and a longing to give thanks for it. We see that every person reaches out for transcendence and goodness that always eludes complete fulfillment but never ceases to beckon. This basic hunger for goodness makes claims on us as teachers and lures us to teach what is more than conceptual knowledge or emotional skills, namely, *how to live well.*

We realize that we do what we do because we feel *called to do it.* It is for us a source of joy. And we give thanks for it.

Reflection: Teaching from Your Heart

Some things to think about from EXPERIENCE:

The poet Rabindranath Tagore wrote,

> I thought that my voyage had come to its end at the last limit of my power—that the path before me was closed, that provisions were exhausted and the time come to take shelter in a silent obscurity. But I find that thy will knows no end in me. And when old words die out on the tongue, new melodies break forth from the heart, and where old tracks are lost, new country is revealed with its wonders.[14]

- Does anything in the above paragraph remind you of teaching?
- Is there any phrase that is especially descriptive of your own experience of teaching?
- Consider recalling this phrase throughout the day to further break open its meaning for yourself.

Now that you have come to the end of this little book, does the following excerpt have any special meaning for you?

> What we call the beginning is often the end
> And to make an end is to make a beginning.
> The end is where we start from...
> With the drawing of this Love and the voice of this
>   Calling
> We shall not cease from exploration
> And the end of all our exploring
> Will be to arrive where we started
> And know the place for the first time.[15]
>   —T. S. Eliot

- Do you agree?
- Have you had a similar insight from your own experience of teaching?

Some things to think about from the SCRIPTURES:

Consider the following passage from the epistles:

> You have been trusted to look after something precious; guard it with the help of the Holy Spirit who lives in us.
> (2 Tim 1:14 JB)

- What is "precious" in your teaching?
- How can you guard it?

Praying about Teaching:

Slowly and prayerfully read the following:

> It is to the glory of my Father that you should bear
>   much fruit,
> and then you will be my disciples.
> As the Father has loved me,
> So I have loved you…
> I have told you this
> so that my own joy may be in you
> and your joy may be complete…
> You did not choose me,
> no, I chose you;
> and I commissioned you
> to go out and to bear fruit,
> fruit that will last;
> and then the Father will give you
> anything you ask him in my name.
> What I command you
> is to love one another.
> (John 15:8–9; 11:16–17 NJB)

AMEN!

NOTES

CHAPTER 1
TEACHING FROM THE HEART:
THE SOUL OF THE TEACHER

1. David T. Hansen, *The Call to Teach* (New York: Teachers College Press, 1995), 6.

2. Parker Palmer, *The Courage to Teach* (San Francisco: Jossey-Bass, 1998), 2.

3. William Butler Yeats, "Among School Children," from *Selected Poems and Two Plays of William Butler Yeats,* ed. M. L. Rosenthal (New York: Collier Books, 1962), 117.

4. From *Tao Te Ching* by Stephen Mitchell. Translation copyright 1988 by Stephen Mitchell (San Francisco: Harper Collins), cited in *Prayers for Healing,* ed. Maggie Oman (Berkeley: Conari Press, 1997), 258.

CHAPTER 2
TEACHING COURAGEOUSLY:
SHOWING HOW

1. Maxine Greene, *Landscapes of Learning* (New York: Teachers College Press, 1978), 3.

2. Jean-Paul Sartre, *Search for a Method* (New York: Knopf, 1968), 94.

3. Parker Palmer, *To Know As We are Known: A Spirituality of Education* (San Francisco: Harper and Row, 1983), 31.

4. Ibid., 71–74.

5. Gabriel Moran, *Showing How: The Act of Teaching* (Valley Forge, Pa.: Trinity Press International, 1997), 68.

6. Ibid., 70.

7. Ibid., 71.

8. Walt Whitman, *Leaves of Grass* (New York: Aventine Press, 1931), 49.

9. See Michael Himes, "The Mission of the Church and Educational Leadership," in *Momentum* (February, 1988): 48 ff. for further discussion of this insight.

10. Ibid.

11. Ascribed to Johann Wolfgang von Goethe (1749–1832), German poet and dramatist.

CHAPTER 3
TEACHING CREATIVELY:
IMAGINING HOW

1. Emily Dickinson, "The Gleam of an Heroic Act," in T. H. Johnson, ed., *The Complete Poems* (Boston: Little, Brown, 1960. Written 1887; originally published 1914) xix–xx.

2. Maurice Merleau-Ponty, *Phenomenology of Perception*, C. Smits, trans. (New York: Humanities Press, 1967) 688–89.

3. Virginia Woolf, *Moments of Being: Unpublished Autobiographical Writings.*, ed. J. Schulkind (Orlando, Fla.: Harcourt, 1976), 72.

4. Maxine Greene, *Releasing the Imagination: Essays on Education, the Arts, and Social Change* (San Francisco: Jossey-Bass, 1995), 28.

5. Sylvia Ashton-Warner, *Teacher* (New York: Simon and Schuster, 1963), 34.

6. Ibid., 99.

7. Ibid., 96.

8. Ibid., 97–98.

9. Erich Fromm, *Escape from Freedom* (New York: Avon Books, 1941), 206–7.

10. Toni Morrison, *Beloved* (New York: Knopf, 1987), 272–73.

11. Maxine Greene, 1995, op. cit., 19.

12. Denis Donoghue, *The Arts without Mystery* (Boston: Little, Brown, 1983), 129.

13. Quoted in Robert Sardello, *Teachers, Teaching and Teacher Education* (Cambridge: Harvard University Press).

14. Ashton-Warner, op. cit., 190–91.

15. Northrup Frye, *The Educated Imagination* (Bloomington: Indiana University Press, 1964), 29.

16. E. E. Cummings, "i thank You God for most this amazing," *100 Selected Poems* (New York: Grove Press, 1959), 114.

CHAPTER 4
TEACHING WISELY:
KNOWING HOW

1. Gabriel Moran, op. cit., 182.

2. Søren Kierkegaard, *Concluding Unscientific Postscript,* trans. David F. Swenson and Walter Lowrie (Princeton: Princeton University Press, 1941), 181.

3. Jose Ortega y Gasset, "The Doctrine of the Point of View," *The Modern Theme* cited in Maxine Greene, *Teacher as Stranger* (1941), 119.

4. Mary Warnock, *Imagination* (Berkeley: University of California Press, 1978), 202.

5. D. H. Lawrence, "Non-Existence," in *The Complete Poems of D. H. Lawrence,* ed. Vivian de Sola Pinto and F. Warren Roberts (New York: Viking Press, 1971), 613.

6. For a fuller discussion of these features, see Parker Palmer, *To Know As We Are Known* (San Francisco: Harper, 1993), 75 ff.

7. John Ciardi, *Manner of Speaking* (New Brunswick, N.J.: Rutgers University Press, 1972).

8. T. S. Eliot, "East Coker," III, in *Collected Poems 1909–1962* (New York: Harcourt, Brace and World, 1963), 187.

CHAPTER 5

TEACHING MORALLY:

THE ETHIC OF CARING

1. Nel Noddings, "Fidelity in Teaching, Teacher Education, and Research for Teaching," *Harvard Educational Review* 56, no. 4 (November, 1980): 384.

2. Aristotle, *Nichomachean Ethics,* book 8, ch. 2, cited in Noddings, op. cit., 498 ff.

3. See Thomas Lickona, *Educating for Character* (New York: Bantam, 1991), for an in-depth presentation of how schools and family can teach children respect and responsibility.

4. Cited in Christina Hoff Sommers, "Teaching the Virtues," *Imprimis* 20, no. 11:4.

5. Ibid., 5.

6. Hansen, op. cit., 123.

7. Nel Noddings, *Caring: A Feminine Approach to Ethics and Moral Education* (Berkeley: University of California Press, 1984), 179 ff.

8. Source unknown.

9. T. S. Eliot, "Ash Wednesday," VI, *Collected Poems 1909–1962* (New York: Harcourt, Brace and World, 1963), 95.

CHAPTER 6:
FACING OURSELVES FACING THE UNFAMILIAR:
MULTIPLE VULNERABILITIES

1. Sylvia Ashton-Warner, op. cit., 198.

2. Ibid.

3. Cited by Wayne Booth in *The Vocation of a Teacher* (Chicago: University of Chicago Press, 1988), 219.

4. Gloria Durka, "Teaching: A Vocation to Community and Tradition," *Momentum* (September 1988): 17.

5. Sylvia Ashton-Warner, op. cit., 87.

6. Nel Noddings, *Caring*, 1984,

7. Henri Nouwen, *Reaching Out* (Garden City, N.Y.: Doubleday, 1975).

8. *The King and I*, paraphrased.

9. Sophie Freud, "The Passion and Challenge of Teaching," in *Teachers, Teaching, and Teacher Education*, ed. Margo Okazawa-Ray, James Anderson, and Robert Traver (Cambridge, Mass.: Harvard University Press, 1987), 130.

10. Ibid., 134.

11. Ibid.

12. Robert Bolt, *A Man for All Seasons*, cited in Frank McNulty, "The Priestly Responsibility to Teach," *Religious Education* 74, no. 2:140.

13. T. S. Eliot, "East Coker," V, *Four Quartets* (1963), 188–89.

14. Cited in *Prayers for Healing*, ed. Maggie Oman (Berkeley: Conari Press, 1997), 218.

CHAPTER 7:
THE JOY OF TEACHING:
A PORTRAIT OF POSSIBILITY

1. Søren Kierkegaard cited in "Defining Common Work," by Kate Olson and T. George Harris, *Ions Connections* 2 (Nov. 1997): 9.

2. T. S. Eliot, "East Coker," III, *Four Quartets,* 187.

3. T. S. Eliot, "Little Gidding," 1, *Four Quartets,* 201.

4. Cited in "The Spirit of Teaching," by Mark R. Schwehn, *Conversations* 10 (fall 1996): 8.

5. Parker Palmer, "Leading from Within," *Noetic Sciences Review* (Winter, 1996): 34.

6. Sartre quoted in Noddings, *Caring,* 140.

7. Rainer Maria Rilke, *Possibility of Being: A Selection of Poems,* trans. J. B. Leishman (New York: New Directions, 1905, 1977), 3.

8. Parker Palmer, *The Company of Strangers* (New York: Crossroad, 1980).

9. Hans Küng, *The Church* (Garden City: Doubleday, 1976).

10. Dwayne Huebner, "Religious Metaphors in the Language of Education," *Religious Education* 80 (Nov. 5, 1985): 464.

11. A. Schutz, *Collected Papers, Vol. 1: The Problem of Social Reality,* 2nd ed. (The Hague: Nijhoff, 1967), 247.

12. Maurice Merleau-Ponty, *Phenomenology of Perception* (Andover, U.K.: International Thomson Publishing Services, Ltd., 1964), 21.

13. Maxine Greene, op. cit., 1995, 86.

14. Rabindranath Tagore, "Gintanjali," XXXVII, in *Collected Poems and Plays of Rabindranath Tagore* (New York: Macmillan, 1958), 14.

15. T. S. Eliot, "Little Gidding," *Four Quartets,* 207–8.